# Home Front
# Killers

First published in 2014

A catalogue record for this book is available from the British Library

ISBN: 978-0-85733-720-7


Published by Haynes Publishing, Sparkford, Yeovil,
Somerset BA22 7JJ, UK
Tel: 01963 442030 Fax: 01963 440001
Int. tel: +44 1963 442030 Int. fax: +44 1963 440001
E-mail: sales@haynes.co.uk
Website: www.haynes.co.uk

Haynes North America Inc., 861 Lawrence Drive, Newbury Park, California 91320, USA

Images © Mirrorpix

Creative Director: Kevin Gardner
Designed for Haynes by BrainWave

Printed and bound in the US

# Home Front Killers

From The Case Files of

**PEOPLE** and **Mirror**

**Claire Welch**

# Contents

# Introduction

A number of crimes took place less frequently during the war years 1914–1918 than we have become used to in the 21$^{st}$ century, continuing the slow growth rates that had endured since the 1870s. However, there was a genuine concern that men who had been so brutalized during the First World War would be immune to violence, and that in the immediate aftermath of war, criminal activities would significantly increase. Theft and robbery did indeed increase, reflecting to an extent the growing opportunities for larceny in a more affluent society, but drunkenness declined significantly, as did murder, which decreased to a level lower than that experienced during Victorian times. It seems that the First World War, the General Strike of 1926 and the mass unemployment that was endured during the Depression had little statistical impact on criminal activity. What did materialize, however, was a media frenzy around "moral panic" and the traditional "right" that was claimed by many men to chastize or to dishonour their wives, in an attempt to re-establish pre-war gender roles. Shell-shock was often deployed as a defence in criminal cases, and for the first time in history, it was recognized that men might suffer mental breakdowns as easily as women.

On the other hand, the advent of the Second World War (1939–1945), actually liberated Britain's criminals: all those with less than three months to serve on their sentences were released from the country's prisons. While various anniversaries are celebrated each year to mark another milestone since atrocities ended, the activities of those who took advantage of war to make their criminal fortunes do not usually receive much publicity. While the nation pulled together, there were those who were far more interested in helping themselves. One of the most notorious criminals was Gordon Cummins, the Black-out Ripper, who murdered four women in London in 1942.

One of the most fascinating insights into civilian life during both world wars is given by Britain's black market and by looting, which became one of the country's growth industries. Crime actually increased by as much as 57 per cent between 1939 and 1945. Britons felt particularly vulnerable to attack during the Second World War and the fall of France was devastating. In fact, until the invasion of Normandy, those on the Home Front felt far more at risk than many British soldiers. It was a terrifying time of uncertainty, but people rallied together to form a committed stronghold in case the Germans invaded. War brought chaos, however, and under this shadow, criminals could operate without fear of too much intervention from the authorities, reprisals or the likelihood of being caught – people were far too preoccupied with necessary sacrifice and safety – although the British people were acutely aware on some levels of the confusion, incompetence and opportunism that accompanied war.

For many, the Home Front presented a new kind of hell that was as dangerous as the battles being fought globally. The Second

World War was a people's war, and no one across the British Isles was unaffected by conflict. Civilian targets were a necessary evil for both the Allies and the Axis and, of course, "ethnic cleansing" was a huge part of atrocities in Germany's occupied territories. Indeed, this threat was a very real part of war throughout Europe. Even in Britain, families of Germans and Italians, to name just two nationalities, who had long settled in the country or were refugees fleeing fascist regimes, suffered as "the enemy", to be feared, mistrusted and treated appallingly badly. War was a reality on a daily basis, with ration books, gas masks, bombings, shelters and the loss of family members – whether at home or abroad. From the Home Guard and children who were being evacuated to women working in industry, everyone was prepared for an invasion. Cities were in the front line, with London, Coventry, Birmingham, Plymouth, Bristol, Hull, Liverpool, Southampton, Manchester, Sheffield, Swansea and Glasgow bearing the brunt of the Luftwaffe's wrath. Inhabitants bravely fought to keep their crumbling cities functioning, and determination was stellar. Many endured the Christmas of 1941 with no gas or electricity, eating cold tinned foods by candlelight, but despite all the bombing, the Germans still failed to invade Britain – and the Führer's orders to advance into Eastern Europe contributed substantially to his eventual downfall. Britain held fast, people continued to rally and determination remained high. Encouraged by Japan's totally unexpected bombing of Pearl Harbor, the US joined the Allies in 1941 at a time when fighting was stepped up in all quarters of the globe, but by the start of 1942, it seemed as if the tide was turning and the long road to victory was beginning. German troops endured extremely harsh conditions during that same year, and at the end of the first month of 1943, the Germans surrendered to the Red Army at Stalingrad.

It was the beginning of the end for atrocities, and the beginning of the end for some burgeoning criminals, although the war years had firmly established the meteoric rise of the criminal underworld. There were many guns on the market following both world wars, although violent crime didn't increase to levels seen in the 19th century and before. However, there was a real concern that (as after the First World War) "citizen soldiers" conscripted into the army would be "dehumanized" and "brutalized" by their experiences, and would return home "morally challenged" and ready to commit heinous, violent crimes. Socially and culturally, attitudes in Britain had been changing for some time, despite the war years, and in terms of criminality, there was a move away from capital punishment, with more emphasis being placed on incarceration and rehabilitation.

"Shell-shock" and the trauma of war were not recognized in quite the same psychological way during the First World War as they were later, and post-traumatic stress was still several generations away. Soldiers during the First World War were removed from the front line, but this was often because they were deemed unpredictable rather than through consideration of their welfare. There has been a great deal of historical interest in crime and the impact of war, but the theory that war creates criminals does not hold true – there is little proof to persuade historians of this fact. Soldiers and civilians alike committed violent crimes – heinous acts were far from the sole domain of men returning from the trenches – but the vast majority of those who returned from fighting were not destined to face the gallows for murder. Some did, of course, but for some former soldiers turned murderers, convictions were either quashed or reduced to manslaughter.

Crime actually decreased during the First World War, although evidence suggests that property crimes increased in Scotland. Crime increased substantially in England, Scotland and Wales during the Second World War, and the black market prospered and grew – the appropriation of goods and supply lines which could so easily be pilfered was, for many, just too tempting. New opportunities for criminal behaviour were undoubtedly provided by war, but whether this actually led to increased violent crime is unclear from historical records. The press, in their endeavours to sensationalize violent crime – particularly murder – during and between the war years, only helped to fuel public opinion that there was a "moral" decline amongst returning veterans. At the time, there was little understanding for the military. The horrors of war were vastly underestimated by those at home, and other criminals who committed heinous crimes did not find themselves the subject of the media frenzy that veterans often endured.

Murder has been a fact of life for centuries, and it seems likely, despite the horrors of war, that very little changed during two world wars. There might have been some murders that went undetected because the focus was elsewhere, but there is also plenty of evidence and proof that murder continued on the Home Front despite the war. In fact, it wasn't just murder on a domestic level that took place. On 24th March 1944, men who were part of "The Great Escape" (which inspired the classic 1963 Hollywood film starring Steve McQueen and Richard Attenborough) were murdered in cold blood on the direct orders of Adolf Hitler. The crime gripped and shocked the nation, and it took a dedicated Blackpool detective to bring the murderers to justice.

Hitler was furious when 76 men broke out of the high-security camp Stalag Luft III and it led to the murder of 50 men. This was the worst war crime against Britain since the 1929 Geneva Convention had been signed to stop such atrocities. Stalag Luft III had deliberately been built to house RAF prisoners of war who had a reputation for ingenuity, aggression and determination. The 24th March 2014 marked the 70th anniversary of the day the Allied airmen tunnelled their way to freedom.

What happened next was equally remarkable, but it remains largely unknown that a team led by a Blackpool detective tracked down the Gestapo men who executed those 50 men, and one by one brought them to justice. When details of the massacre filtered back home, Foreign Secretary Anthony Eden, later Prime Minister, vowed to track down the murderers. Of the 76 men who had escaped in March 1944, only three got back to Britain; the rest had been caught, and Hitler had ordered the execution of 50 of them. Told to relieve themselves before a long drive back to the camp, men from 12 nations were shot in the back as they stepped away, and their bodies were cremated. After the war the Germans responsible were scattered across Europe, and many changed their names. The job of tracking them down was given to a team led by Detective Frank McKenna, who had served in Bomber Command and was nicknamed "Sherlock Holmes".

He and his team received their mission nearly 18 months after the event, with no crime scene to investigate, no witnesses and no obvious starting point. It was more than duty that drove McKenna to succeed. Two of the men shot in cold blood were his friends, Flight Lieutenant Edgar Humphreys and Flying Officer Robert Stewart, who had been stationed at RAF Squires Gate in Blackpool. His own brother-in-law Howard Luck had also been on the escape list at Stalag Luft III but was turned back because of a lack of time for preparation. That disappointment saved his life.

Speaking for the first time about Frank McKenna's mission, his son Ian said: "This was personal for him. He also knew how easily he could have ended up in a camp like that. Those men were only doing their duty by escaping and he wanted to bring their killers to justice." Handed a "most wanted" list of missing Nazis, the team began searching for leads at record offices and prison camps. At one camp they read of so many Nazi atrocities that they felt sick. The first breakthrough came in a tip-off from a Hamburg hotelier who was suspicious of a guest claiming to be French. In fact he was Ernst Kah, head of the SS intelligence division and No. 12 on the list. Eager to prove his co-operation, he rattled off the names of other Nazis and where to look for them.

Slowly but surely McKenna's team made progress. Some Gestapo members were found in Allied prisons under false identities. One even worked for the US Army. Erich Zacharias had shot Canadian Flying Officer Gordon Kidder, and also raped and murdered an 18-year-old Czech receptionist who overheard him beating an RAF prisoner. He was also cited as having murdered British Squadron Leader Thomas Kirby-Green but other reports claim that he didn't: that the squadron leader was shot by Gestapo agent Adolf Knüppelberg. The Allies had labelled Zacharias "harmless" and given him a job as a customs clerk in the port of Bremen. McKenna surprised him on his shift and arrested him on the spot. He carried a 9mm Beretta machine carbine, which had been given to him by an American colonel who was horrified that McKenna was driving around Europe with no firearms. Zacharias had to be recaptured twice. First he escaped from US custody, but McKenna acted quickly and found him at home, packing. Then in England he dug his way out of jail, but was recaptured again. In the UK, the *Mirror* headline read: "Gestapo Man Hunted in London: 'Dangerous'." Sam Jackett, the evening news reporter wrote: "Thousands of police in London and the Home Counties were today hunting a dangerous German prisoner of war – a member of the Gestapo – who bolted at

1.00am today from his cell at Kempton Park racecourse prison camp, where he was being held in connection with the murder of 50 RAF men at Stalag Luft III, at Sagan ... As soon as the man was missed from his cell, the War Office called in Scotland Yard, and the missing man's description was radioed to cars throughout London. A police cordon was thrown around London in record time. All cars and lorries were stopped and searched. Every officer now engaged in the hunt has been told that the escaped prisoner, Erik Zacharias, believed to have been a former member of the Gestapo is 'dangerous'."

While waiting for the gallows, Zacharias gave McKenna a Rolex watch, which in 2014 was worth £10,000. Ian said: "He told my father: 'You are the only one who has been really fair to me. Everyone else has beaten me up but you never did. I want you to have my watch as a thank you for treating me well.' My dad never ill-treated his prisoners, and that must have taken great self control."

McKenna also showed kindness when he arrested Emil Schulz, the man who shot the Great Escape plot's leader Flight Commander Roger Bushell – the inspirational character played by Richard Attenborough in the film. McKenna soon realized that Schulz had little time for the Nazis, and only murdered Bushell because he would have been killed if he had disobeyed. Although he delivered him to be sentenced and executed, McKenna secretly agreed to deliver a final message to the man's widow.

The painstaking investigation took two years and over

100,000 interviews. By 1948 the team had arrested 44 Gestapo men, including Johannes Post, a particularly notorious Nazi who led the executions and took sadistic pleasure in them. Thirty were tried, 13 executed and 17 jailed. Three were acquitted, and 11 killed themselves while awaiting trial.

Frank McKenna was awarded an OBE, but his role was never well known. He went back to his detective work in Blackpool, a role that had initially kept him out of the war: he had volunteered early on but worked in a restricted profession. It was only when Bomber Command began to suffer huge casualties that men like him were allowed to enlist in that most dangerous of units. By then, he and wife Eunice had suffered a personal tragedy. Their eldest son Terry (9) was hit by a car and killed in 1941. Ian, a toddler at the time, said: "Dad was so bereft he visited Terry's grave every day. He never really recovered from it." McKenna joined the RAF and beat the odds to survive more than 30 missions as a flight engineer. Ian said: "Before my mum died she told me they talked it over and Dad said it was the right thing to do. Bits of what was happening in the Holocaust were starting to filter through and he said it was his duty."

Frank died aged 87 in 1994. A month later he was honoured with a speech at a memorial service to mark the 50th anniversary of the Great Escape at the RAF church at St Clement Danes, London. His old RAF friend Charles Hobgen said: "Frank never sang his own praises but he never tired of praising those who worked with him on the Stalag Luft III investigation. They created a forensic legend that time must not be permitted to dim."

Other murders during the war years were just as heinous. Alongside single murderers such as Gordon Cummins were killers such as John Reginald Christie, responsible for the murder of at least eight women, John George Haigh, known as the "Acid Bath" murderer, George Joseph Smith, known for "The Brides in the Bath" murders, and Joseph Spooner, who was executed in Liverpool in 1915 by prolific executioner Albert Pierrepoint for the murder of his three-year-old daughter.

*Home Front Killers* takes a look at the stories that hit the headlines during the First and Second World Wars, and uncovers criminal activities on British soil during wartime, as well as the emergence of the criminal underworld, its leading gangsters and the opportunities seized by many during the Blitz and the blackouts.

# Donald Lesbini
1914

Charged with murdering Alice Storey – having shot her on Tottenham Court Road in London – Donald Lesbini, a "deserter" from the Worcestershire Regiment, was remanded at Marlborough Street on 13th August 1914. "Death Sentence on a Deserter" read the headline on 12th September that year. The article in the *Mirror* said: "Sentence of death was passed, at the Old Bailey yesterday, on Donald Lesbini, a tutor, aged twenty-two, an army deserter, who was found guilty of the murder of Alice Storey.

"The girl was an attendant at 'Fairyland', Tottenham Court-road, and he shot her with a revolver, because, he said, she insulted him by calling him 'Ikey.' Evidence was given that as a boy [the] prisoner's condition was one of mental irresponsibility. Mr Dyer, of Brixton Prison, said [the] prisoner lacked mental balance, but there were no symptoms of insanity about him."

During the First World War, Fairyland was a shooting range, owned and managed by Henry Stanley Morley.

This case established new laws in the UK, Canada and Australia with regard to voluntary manslaughter. Lesbini was later reprieved, but his mental health deteriorated, and in 1931 he was sent to Broadmoor. "Ikey" was a racial slur, used to describe a Jew – and Lesbini had taken offence at it being used against him.

# Open Verdict on Baby Deaths

1915

A baby, aged about 10 days old, had been found dead in the Regent's Canal, near Kingsland Road Bridge, the coroner's jury at Shoreditch heard on 5th January 1915. The infant, the coroner concluded, had been murdered by some person or persons unknown. There had been a similar verdict a fortnight before with regard to another baby's death. The tiny infant had been found strangled in a parcel in Shaftesbury Street, London. Dr Albert M. Balow said there were no external marks of violence, and the child, which had been quite healthy, had been dead for about a week before it was found. He was certain that it did not die naturally, but it was difficult to say whether death was due to drowning or suffocation. The coroner asked: "It must have been a wilful murder?" "Yes," said the witness. The coroner advised the jury to return an open verdict on the second baby, and said that "no doubt the police would endeavour strenuously" to trace the parents in both cases.

# Sidney Clements
## 1915

A 15-year-old boy was found guilty of murder on 13th January 1915. Sidney Clements, described as an office boy, stood in the dock at the Old Bailey, convicted of the murder of his seven-year-old stepbrother.

"This extraordinary boy seems to have had the question of murder by youths under sixteen in his mind," said Mr Muir, prosecuting. He continued: "Because in October last, while walking with a friend, they were talking about a boy aged seventeen who, it was said, had been hanged for murder." The accused was alleged to have asked: "If a boy of fourteen or fifteen was to kill anyone would he be hung?" The friend replied: "No, he would be sent to a reformatory school for about fifteen years."

The boy, Counsel continued, had a grievance against his stepmother because she took his earnings of about 8s a week for the use of the family. On the evening of 16th November 1914, she left for the evening and both boys stayed at the family home. When she returned, she found her young son had been stabbed with a carving knife. Sidney Clements had disappeared with two savings bank books, and later he wrote from Southend: "Dear Dad.- I am very, very sorry for what I done to Bert, but I hope he is all right. When I was cleaning knives and forks I seemed to have gone mad all of a sudden and done what I did do. And now I can hardly realize what I done. I am always thinking it was a dream instead of being true."

Addressing the young lad, the judge, Mr Justice Rowlatt, said: "Clements, you have been found guilty of a wicked … cowardly act towards a poor little child. If you had been a little older you would have been well and deservedly hanged, and if you ever do the like again after you come out of the place of detention to which you will be sent, hanged you will be." The judge ordered that the youth be detained "during His Majesty's pleasure".

# George Smith
# (Brides in the Bath)

1915

In the early part of the 20<sup>th</sup> century, newspaper headlines were followed, on average, by two sub-headings. The first mention of George Smith on 3<sup>rd</sup> February 1915 was no different. "TALE OF TWO BRIDES DEAD IN BATHS," read the first headline. "Story of 'Phenomenal Coincidence' in Charge Against Agent" and "That is my hard luck," read the next two. The article began: "A remarkable story of a man who married twice and whose two wives were found dead in their baths, the first a few weeks after her wedding and the second on the day following her marriage, was told at Bow-street Police Court yesterday."

In the dock stood George Smith (43), described as a "land agent". He was charged with "causing to be inserted in a marriage register a false entry relating to a marriage between himself as John Lloyd and Margaret Lofty at the Register Office, Bath, on December 17 last". Detective Inspector Neil stated that the previous day he had seen the "prisoner" in Uxbridge Road. Mr Neil said to Smith: "Are you John Lloyd?" The accused answered in the affirmative. "You were married to Margaret Lofty at Bath … and she was found dead by you in a bath at 14 Bismarck-road, Highgate, the following evening?" Smith replied: "Yes, quite right." Mr Neil then said: "You are also said to be identical with George Smith, whose wife was found dead in a bath under similar circumstances on December 13, 1913, at Blackpool, and whom you married a few weeks before." George Smith allegedly vehemently denied that he was Smith, and told the detective he had no idea what he was talking about. However, when this was mentioned in court, he said: "You are telling lies – I said: 'Quite right.'" Mr Neil, taking no notice of Smith, told the police court that he had told the "prisoner" that if it was found that he was George Smith he would be charged with making a false entry. Smith replied: "In that case, I may as well say my proper name is George Smith and my wife died at Blackpool. The entry in the register [at Bath] is not correct, but that is the only charge you have against me." Mr Neil continued: "I said to him: 'The question of further charges is a matter of inquiry.'" George Smith said: "Well, I must admit that two deaths like that form a phenomenal coincidence. But that is my hard luck."

Smith was sent by police to Kentish Town police station, and was later required to take part in an identity parade. Mr Burnham, father of the first victim, and Mrs Pinchin, her sister, both hesitated before identifying Smith. He was then charged with making the "false entry" in Bath, and in response said: "All right. This is the only charge you can put against me and that is what I am guilty of. My wife [referring to the woman he married in Bath] knew all about my first marriage, and she suggested I should make a fresh start and say nothing of my former wife, as I had told her how she died. It was against my interests to give the name of Lloyd, as I had an annuity of £2 in the name of Smith from the North British and Mercantile Insurance Company." He had, however, taken some possessions, banknotes and cash, including the annuity, although the newspapers didn't give specific details as to when or where. Smith gave his address as Richmond Road, Shepherd's Bush, before being remanded in custody.

At the inquest into Alice Smith's death on 13th December 1913 in Blackpool, Smith gave evidence, weeping as he explained how he had only known his wife, who had been a nurse, for three months. They had been married for six weeks. He said that his wife had complained of a pain in her head and he took her to see a doctor who gave her medication, but she complained again of headaches two days later. Smith told the inquest that he took his wife for a walk, after which she said she felt better. It was her idea to have a bath, he said. About 20 minutes after she had gone into the bathroom he called out to her and received no answer. The door was unlocked, and he entered the room to find his wife lying underneath the water. He held her head above water until the doctor arrived. Dr George Billing said that a post-mortem revealed that death was due to drowning. He believed that a heart condition had caused Mrs Smith to faint while in the bath, and a verdict of "accidentally drowned" was recorded.

On 4th February 1915 it was announced that the bodies of both wives were to be exhumed by order of the Home Office. Margaret Elizabeth Lloyd was exhumed at Islington Cemetery,

East Finchley, under the cover of darkness in the presence of three police officers. The grave was unmarked, and it took the gravediggers, working by the dim light of lanterns, until 11.30pm to bring her coffin to the surface. After the police, by a glance at the plate, had confirmed it was the deceased woman's, it was lowered to just below the surface, where it rested on a temporary staging. The grave was then covered with boards and guarded by police. At 7.30am officers arrived with an undertaker's hearse so that the coffin could be taken away.

Five days later, there were dramatic scenes at Bow Street police court when Smith again appeared. Described as tall and sparely built with sharp features, he made several "dramatic" interruptions while evidence was being given by Detective Inspector Neil. Defending, Mr Davies asked the inspector if he had told the accused that the bodies would be exhumed. Mr Neil denied that he had said anything, but Smith said: "You did say so. You said I did it on purpose to get the insurance money. I told you I received the insurance money under another name. That is why I said it." Intervening, Mr Hopkins, the magistrate, said: "Do you not think, Mr Davies, that this is a rather dangerous line to take at this stage?" Smith allegedly told officers at Bow Street, where he was being held, that he had nothing to fear and his conscience was clear. The hearing was adjourned.

On behalf of the Director of Public Prosecutions, Mr Archibald Bodkin said that Smith stated at his second marriage that he was John Lloyd, bachelor, land agent. On the night of their marriage,

Smith and Mrs Lloyd had rented an apartment from Miss Blatch, in Islington, London. The circumstances surrounding Mrs Lloyd's death demanded an inquest, according to the coroner. Bodkin said: "At that inquest prisoner gave evidence in the name of John Lloyd. He was not, in fact, a bachelor, as he stated to the registrar; he was a widower, and his name is George Joseph Smith. The way in which the evidence will prove that is that it appears that in the year before ... prisoner was at Southsea, living at 80 Kimberley Road.

"There he made the acquaintance of a woman named Miss Alice Burnham, who was employed at Southsea, and as Mr George Smith he, on November 4, 1913, at the register office, Portsmouth, was married to her.

"About five or six weeks after the marriage – on December 10, 1913 – prisoner and his wife went to Blackpool and took lodgings at the house of Mrs Crossley, and on December 13, Mrs Smith died." Bodkin continued: "At the inquest which was held prisoner gave his name as George Joseph Smith ... Thus when he went through the ceremony at Bath he was not John Lloyd, and he was not a bachelor." William Winkworth, the registrar from Bath, was then called. He knew that Smith had given the name of Lloyd, but had not been present at the marriage.

The case came before magistrates again on 15th February 1915, and again, Smith was remanded. The only witness that day was William Hayward, the registrar for marriages in Bath, who had been present at the marriage. Smith was remanded for another week until 22nd February, when the only witness was Thomas Bird, the clerk who had been present at the inquest into the death of Mrs Lloyd. Prosecuting, Mr Bodkin stated that Detective Inspector Neil was still making inquiries. In early March 1915, the prosecutor told a subsequent hearing that there was evidence to support a "very much graver charge". Meanwhile, Charles Pleasants, an inspector for the North British and Mercantile Insurance Company, confirmed that Smith had asked for his company's rates. He had met both Mr and Mrs Smith and not long afterwards received a letter in which "the writer announced the death of his wife". Detective Reed, who searched Smith's lodging in Shepherd's Bush, had found a suspicious empty bottle. Mr Davies was ordered by the magistrate to keep his client "quiet" after he interjected while the witness was giving his evidence. The police court then heard that Smith had said: "My conscience is clear. I am wrong about the register, but it has got to be proved that it was with felonious intent before they can do anything with me. If she had not been insured nothing would have been said, and I did not know she was insured. The policy was sent to me; it was sent anonymously to my address at Highgate." According to newspaper reports, Detective Sergeant Page remarked after Smith's arrest that he had said: "You may think it strange, but it was the irony of fate that my two wives should have died in the same way. I suppose this has come about through the insurance. I did not know she was insured till after she was dead, nor that she had made a will. Someone at

Bristol, no, Bath, sent the papers to me. That was the first time I knew about the insurance. I suppose this trouble would have come when my first wife died if she had been insured."

Smith remained in custody. On 9th March the case saw dramatic developments when he heard the prosecutor say: "I shall be able to call evidence of the marriage of the prisoner in 1898 and the continued existence of his wife now living, and also of several other marriages since that time. His first wife's maiden name was Caroline Beatrice Thornhill." New evidence was then presented to show that Smith had contracted three other marriages in the names of Love, Williams and James. His first marriage had taken place on 17th January 1898 in St Matthew's Church, Leicester. Smith was known as George Oliver Love when he married Caroline Thornhill – who later emigrated to Canada. The second marriage in Weymouth – where he used the name Williams – was to Miss Munday in August 1910. His third marriage took place in Woolwich Register Office on 17th September 1914, when he called himself Oliver Charles James and "married" Alice Beatrice Reavill. Caroline Thornhill's mother gave evidence to the court that Smith was the man who married her daughter. "Yes" was her reply when asked if it was Smith. Turning towards the dock, she pointed one of her hands to the prisoner and, controlling herself with an effort, cried: "And that man knows it!" Smith had listened intently to the proceedings before being held on remand yet again. The sexton of St Matthew's, Arthur Elliott, also recognized Smith; he particularly recognized his voice.

Giving her evidence, Mrs Thornhill said that her daughter had been 17 at the time of the marriage and that she didn't approve of the union. She told the court that "Love" and her daughter lived in a baker's shop for three months after the marriage, but two years later he took a haberdasher's shop in Martin Street, Leicester. The couple lived there for four months, but then her daughter returned home. Frederick Crabb from Weymouth also recognized the prisoner as the man who had lived with a Miss Munday in the apartments he rented out in the town. Mr Crabb and his wife were witnesses at the register office, but Smith left the town the following month and was never seen in Weymouth again. Cyril James, the registrar of marriages in Woolwich, recognized Smith as the man who married Alice Reavill.

Alice told the court that she had met Smith while on holiday in Bournemouth. He introduced himself as Charles Oliver James and told her he was an artist. They met a few times before he proposed marriage, and she accepted. She returned to her home in Plumstead in September and they were married later that month. Alice confirmed in court that she had "possessed some property". She said: "I had a number of things. He suggested that I should sell them and I got £14 for them. He asked me to give the money to him, but I said I was quite capable of looking after it myself, and would not hand it over.

"At the time we were married I had the money, and afterwards as we were driving from Waterloo to Clapham in a cab, he asked me for the money. He showed me banknotes which, he said, amounted to £72. I did not inspect them but handed over my money. When we got to Clapham and the luggage was taken upstairs he came down with a Post Office Savings Bank withdrawal form and asked me to sign it. He knew that I had money there, and after we were married he said he would like me to draw it out, so as to make a banking account of it.

"We went out together and posted the form. It was for £72 and some odd silver. The warrant arrived after a day or two, and he came with me to the bank to get it. He asked for the money in £1 notes, but they said they could not do it. There was interest on the money which brought it to £76. There were five £10 and some £5 and £1 notes, but he took those and I did not see the rest . . . I took only the odd money."

The next morning the couple left their lodgings to look for a house. They took the tram and "James" asked Alice if she would like to visit Halifax in Nova Scotia. When they got off the tram they passed through some gardens. "James" then told his wife: "I shall not be many minutes; wait here." Alice waited for an hour, but never saw her husband again. She lost all her money. She returned to the lodgings, having nowhere else to go, and discovered a telegram from Smith: "Dearest – I could not possibly let you know beforehand of my programme, otherwise you might not have agreed to have come together until my return from Halifax, but I am due at Halifax, Canada, next Friday. Also I could not bear to come and say goodbye before going, because you would, perhaps, have broken down and tried to stop me from going. So I thought it best to do it this way.

"I have a splendid home there awaiting you. If you will forgive me, do come to Halifax as soon as possible. There will be no more obstacles in our way then, and you will be the happiest woman in the world. I have placed certain money in your luggage and directed it to your house at Woolwich ... Cheer up! All's well that ends well. C James, The Avenue, Halifax ... will find me. Everyone knows me there – Charles."

Alice never got her luggage. On 23rd March 1915 the *Mirror* stated that Smith was to be charged with the murder of three women. Prosecuting counsel brought the news in a "dramatic" statement he made to the court. The newspaper described Smith as a man with a "greed for wealth", while the prosecution accused him of being "daring". Smith was thought to have gained more than £2,800 from the death of two of his "wives", but at the time of his arrest was expected to lay his hands on at least a further £700. It was revealed that in 1906 Smith had "married" a woman named Pegler. Each time Smith had "married", events that had resulted in three deaths, the relationships had followed the same pattern: an illicit "courtship" followed on Smith's part by "pretended affection", a bigamous marriage and persuasion to make a will, with the accused the sole "legatee", before death in the bath. All three women died as a result of drowning. Each one had then been "discovered" by Smith and each woman's family had received a letter from the killer. In each case, the coroner's jury recorded an accidental death.

In 1910, Smith was absent from the home he shared with his "wife" Edith Pegler, and wrote to her that he was in Weymouth. It was here that he met Constance Annie Munday, known as Bessie, whom he then married. She died on 13<sup>th</sup> July 1912 at Herne Bay. The daughter of a Wiltshire bank manager, who had left his property to her and his son, Bessie's income was around £100 a year, and she lived a rather solitary life in boarding houses. In August 1910, she sent a letter to her uncle, which was followed by another from Smith. Within three days of the marriage Smith wrote to the uncle again, requesting that all Bessie's money should be forwarded to him. On 13<sup>th</sup> September, he told his landlady he had to go to London on important business, and that when his wife returned (she had gone out for the day) to tell her if he wasn't back that night he would be home on the following Monday. He didn't return for Bessie until 18 months later, but returned in the meantime to Edith. They lived in Southend, Barking and Bristol. Miss Munday then went to live in Weston-super-Mare, and was reconciled with Smith in March 1912. There were still other "wives" at this point whom the authorities and the press did not know about. Smith and Munday travelled to Woolwich before moving to Herne Bay. There was no bath at their house, and Smith enquired about the price of one; a new one was delivered on 5<sup>th</sup> July. On 8<sup>th</sup> July, Bessie left all her money to her "husband". Smith twice called on Dr French in the days before Bessie's death to talk to him about the "fits" that his wife had been suffering: she had never had fits before and they didn't run in her family. On 13th July, Smith sent a note to the doctor saying: "Do come at once. I am afraid my wife is dead." Dr French found Bessie Munday in the bath, her head submerged. The water was tepid and the woman was dead. Counsel said: "Although three parts full, that is, holding forty-one gallons of water and counting two gallons to two buckets, this woman, who had been suffering from fits, would have to make some twenty journeys up to that bedroom to fill that bath three-parts full of water, and the story that her head was down under the water is one which I submit is impossible to believe, unless it had been forced under the water by some such methods of raising, for instance, the legs. If that was done the head and shoulders would then naturally slide down the sloping parts at the head of the bath.

"The bath is here in court, and, taking into consideration the build, the height and the physical appearance of Miss Munday, it will be a question for you to say whether any such thing as a fit ever occurred, or any faintness or collapse occurred, so as to allow such a woman to sink beneath the water of a bath three-parts full, and beneath the surface of the water in such a bath – impossible. There is a remarkable thing which is common in all these three cases. The woman is going to have a bath, she undresses, and leaves the door unfastened. Each one of these women when they wanted to take what one might call their fatal bath, although two of them are in strange houses in which they have never been before, they open the door of the bathroom.

Anyone who knows anything about the character of a woman would indeed require to be satisfied that that was accidental; that three wives, in three houses, are going to take three baths, and each die in that bath, and the door unfastened."

Smith, said Mr Bodkin, paid a visit to the clerk of the owner of 80 High Street, Herne Bay. He went into the office, laid his head on the desk and wept. The clerk asked him what was the matter and he said his wife was dead. She had drowned in the bath, which was a large one and which she had bought herself. Then he looked up at the clerk and said: "Was it not a jolly good job I got her to make her will?" The clerk was reported as having been disgusted.

Mr Bodkin next addressed the death of Alice Burnham, who married Smith before her death in Blackpool. Smith wrote to the 25-year-old woman's father asking for £100, "which you have been minding for her", and asked that the sum, made up from Alice's own savings and a £40 gift from her father, should be forwarded to him. The couple arrived in Blackpool and were about to take a room in Mrs Marsden's house in Adelaide Street when Smith asked: "Is there a bathroom?" Mrs Marsden told him that there wasn't, and Smith replied: "Well this will not do for us if there is no bathroom." They took rooms with Mrs Crossley in 16 Regent Road instead, and Alice complained of a headache on their first evening. She was taken by her husband to see Dr Billings, who diagnosed "maziness" (being perplexed or confused) and prescribed some medication. It was a parallel, said the prosecution, with the scene at Herne Bay. There it was noticed that a quantity of water was running down the walls and through the ceiling to the kitchen, as if quite a considerable amount of water had been spilt in the bathroom. Alice "Smith" was found in the bath the wrong way round, with her feet at the sloping end and her head towards the plughole. When asked by the doctor why he hadn't let the water out of the bath, Smith said he hadn't thought of it. He wasn't at all fazed that he would have to sleep in the room where his wife's dead body lay, and the prosecution suggested that this indicated how callous Smith was. Alice was not wearing her rings at the time she was discovered, and Smith was later seen slipping them from the mantel into his coat pocket by the landlady. Hairpins were found in Alice's hair, indicating she had had no intention of getting her hair wet, and there was hair on both sides of the bath, indicating signs of a struggle.

Counsel then turned its attention to Margaret Lofty. Her bath was requested by the murdered woman herself and prepared by the landlady, who had seen Smith trying to lift Margaret out of the bath. Miss Lofty was 5ft 3in tall and the bath was just slightly longer at 5ft 6in. Bruises were found on her elbow. Counsel read a letter found in the dead woman's clothing: "No doubt you are surprised to know I am married … He is a thoroughly Christian man. Our tastes and temperaments and so forth were always in harmony … He is such a nice man, I am perfectly happy." However, Mr Bodkin said he needed to deal with the medical side of the evidence at length.

Smith, as at each of the previous hearings, was prone to interrupting court proceedings when he disagreed with the prosecution's case. On 29th March 1915 he brought the session to a halt when he cried out: "I am on a charge for my life ... and it is my business to protect it. This has been made up by the detectives ... I never said a word about the bath ... I can tolerate the truth, but I cannot stand this." However, "dramatic" evidence was given by Miss Blatch about the bath that Mrs Lloyd took. She described how she prepared the bath and then heard someone going upstairs. Mr Bodkin said: "And after you heard someone go upstairs, what was the next thing you heard?" The court waited in silence before Miss Blatch said: "I heard some splashing in the bath ... and that was about ten minutes after I had heard somebody go upstairs." She was asked what the splashing was like and paused before replying: "I heard a noise like arms knocking against the side of the bath. Then I heard a sigh. It was just like a sigh that would come from a baby that was having a bath or having its face washed." The magistrate asked if it was like a "recovery of the breath", to which she answered: "Yes. I do not know whether the sound came from the bathroom. There seemed to be a noise too, like wet hands being slapped against something." The next thing that Miss Blatch heard was the organ being played for about 10 minutes. After that she heard the front door bang, then the doorbell rang. It was Smith, who claimed he had popped out to buy tomatoes for Mrs Lloyd's supper but had forgotten to take his key with him. He then went a little way up the stairs before calling to Margaret. There was no answer so he proceeded up the stairs. He called to Miss Blatch to come and help him, and when she arrived – having first tried to find another tenant but with no luck – she saw him lifting his wife out of the bath, although her legs were still inside it. She insisted that she should fetch a policeman and the doctor, and Smith asked her to call for Dr Bates. Smith was again alleged to have asked other witnesses whether rooms had a bath. He denied this vehemently. Rising from his seat in the dock, he shouted: "I cannot sit here and hear this. This is a lot of lies. This has been made up by the detectives." Mr Davies was asked to keep his client quiet, but Smith continued to rant, saying that the female witness had been paid to tell the court lies by the police: "You are paid for this. I never said a word about the bath. Bribery, nothing but bribery." As Detective Inspector Neil passed the dock, Smith turned to him and shouted: "You pay these people to say this, you dirty tyke. It is all invention and nothing else." PC Russett then produced plans of the house where Margaret died. The witness after the dead woman's sister, who had not seen the accused before the hearing and had no knowledge of her sister's plans to marry, was Emma Heiss, who lived next door to the house in Highgate. She told the court that on 4th December she had answered a knock at the door from a man – she identified Smith – who asked for a sitting room and bedroom for himself and his wife. He was alleged to have asked if there was a bathroom. She showed him the bathroom on the landing and he said: "This is a very small bath." But Smith took exception to the woman's testimony, and cried out that she was a liar. Louisa Blatch also confirmed that Smith had inquired about a bathroom before agreeing to take a bedroom on the second floor and a sitting room on the ground floor. That first night Margaret had complained of a headache and gone to bed early. She asked for her fateful bath the following day.

The case was resumed on 8th April 1915 at Bow Street, and for the first time since the trial began a number of well-known people attended, including Lord Ribblesdale and his daughter, Sir Arthur Pinero, the dramatist, and Mr H.B. Irving, the actor, alongside Sir Robert Peel. On the night Margaret died, Smith was said to have asked whether her body could be removed. PC Heath was called to the scene shortly after the body was found, and told the court: "I saw the prisoner kneeling beside the body of a woman lying on the floor." Smith was alleged to have been "working" the arms backwards and forwards. Mr Bodkin said: "Did you speak to the prisoner at all?" The police constable remembered saying: "Is she dead?" to which Smith replied: "She must have been in the bath about an hour." Smith claimed to PC Heath that he was trying to revive his wife.

More witnesses of the death of Miss Munday were heard, including a Mrs Tuckett, originally from Weston-super-Mare, who stated that the murdered woman had lived with her for a time. Smith was introduced to her as Miss Munday's husband. He had later written the landlady a letter: "As far as Bessie and I are concerned, not only is the past forgiven, but forgotten. Not only has Bessie said so on oath before the solicitors, but she has given the promise to me in a letter, which I shall always prize. Thus my future object in life will be to prove myself not only a true husband and gentleman, but, finally, to make my peace, step by step, with all that have been kind to Bessie. Why, in the name of Heaven and Christianity, should people try to stir up past troubles."

Hearings continued in what had been dubbed by the press "The Dead Bride's Case". On 21st April Smith accused Detective Sergeant Reed of "grinning" at him during proceedings. He had continued to interrupt witnesses giving evidence, and shouted at Reed: "More of your business I suppose. Call yourself a man? Nothing but bribery." That day also heard Margaret Crossley describe how she had noticed water coming through the ceiling of her house in Blackpool. Smith had entered the kitchen below the bathroom, and had told Mrs Crossley that he and his wife would have eggs for breakfast the following day. He then shouted up to his wife to turn out the light once she had finished in the bathroom. When Alice was found dead, Smith seemed unperturbed, and Mrs Crossley accused him that night of being a callous man. From the dock Smith denied that she had ever said this, and the witness, ignoring him, said that she had found him a bed elsewhere that night. Smith wanted to stay in the house with his wife, telling Mrs Crossley that: "When they are dead they are dead." She made him leave.

The court heard how Smith was prone to choosing public

graves – as provided for the penniless – for his wives rather than private burial sites. He told the undertaker in Blackpool that he wanted a moderate funeral because: "I don't want to throw money away." He also told the man that "when she was dead she was done with". Smith rose angrily in the dock and denied that any such conversations had ever taken place. On 6th May, Smith appeared in the dock for the eighteenth time. Charles Pleasants was cross-examined by Mr Sherman for the defence, who put it to him that he had tried to persuade Miss Burnham to insure her life. Pleasants denied that he had. He also denied that he had promised the prisoner half of the commission on the policy on the woman's life.

Two days later, Frederick Eccleshall, a solicitor from Cheltenham, told the court that in November 1914, Smith had visited him with the will of his wife Alice – and was instructed to obtain certain policies which amounted to £500. But Smith lashed out, demanding to know what the witness' evidence had to do with murder. Meanwhile, a bank clerk in Bristol confirmed that Smith had opened a new account. Again, Smith demanded to know how this was relevant.

On 12th May 1915, after more than 100 witnesses had been heard over hearings totalling 19 days, George Smith was committed for trial by Sir John Dickinson on three charges of murder. The magistrate intimated that the murder of Margaret would be committed to the Old Bailey, the murder of Bessie to Maidstone and Alice's murder to Lancaster. A grand jury was likely to be asked to consider each case in each area before the whole case was transferred to the Old Bailey. Dr Bernard Spilsbury, the officiating pathologist, gave evidence after examining the bodies of all three women. He had found recent bruises on the body of Margaret that could have been made before she drowned, but owing to her size he did not think her head could have become submerged during an epileptic fit. He also did not know how Bessie could have got herself into the position she was found in, with her legs straight out from the hips and her feet out of the water. He also did not think that Alice's natural hair would have been found in the bath in great quantities if she had died in the way her husband had described.

On 16th June 1915, the Recorder at the Old Bailey said: "Every one of these unfortunate women, if they met their deaths in the way suggested by foul play at the prisoner's hands, lost their lives purely for the prisoner to obtain sums of money." He also said that Smith was charged with bigamy and "making a false declaration in the register", and that there had been other cases of bigamy. He added that the grand jury would probably agree with him that a "true bill" (if it found cause to make a charge) should be found. Later that day, after deliberating, the grand jury agreed. Smith's trial at the Old Bailey was fixed for later in June.

The case caused a public outcry, and there was huge interest in the trial which began on 22nd June 1915. Prosecuting were Mr Bodkin, Travers Humphreys and Cecil Whiteley. Sir Edward Marshall Hall, KC, and Mr M. Shearman defended on the instructions of Mr Davies. There was a great deal of excitement as Smith entered the courtroom and made his way to the dock. "Not guilty," he replied in a firm voice, when asked how he pleaded to the charge of murdering Miss Munday. Then he sat down.

Mr Bodkin's opening speech lasted more than seven hours, during which time Smith sat with his arms folded. Bodkin said: "There is a simple, but terribly effective way in which a person in a bath could be drowned, and that is, if somebody had lifted the legs, the immediate effect would be that the trunk of the body would go down the sloping part and there would be almost immediate unconsciousness and rapid and silent death the inevitable result." He also gave details of Smith's early career – in the name of Love – and talked of his first marriage in 1898. It was communicated in court that Mrs Thornhill had travelled from Canada to attend the trial. The details of how Smith and Bessie Munday met and conducted their relationship – along with the letters sent to her uncle – were then outlined, as well as the fact that Smith could benefit financially only following her death. Mr Bodkin then told the jury of the circumstances surrounding the deaths of Alice and Margaret, and concluded: "There are numerous points of similarity in the three cases which justify the grave assertion that the prisoner was out to make money out of drowning people with whom he went through an apparent form of marriage." The judge decided that the cases of murder of Alice and Margaret could be "produced as bearing on the question" as to whether Smith murdered the women to obtain money.

Bessie's brother, George Munday, had received a letter from Smith telling him his sister had died. He immediately wrote back to the accused telling him that as she had died so suddenly he felt a post-mortem should be carried out. Smith was said to have replied to the letter by saying that he was surprised Mr Munday thought a post-mortem was necessary, and concluded that "he was too hurt to say more".

Later in the trial, one of the jurymen suggested that if someone could be placed in the bath in which Bessie died – it had been brought in as an exhibit – it would better demonstrate what allegedly occurred. The judge made his feelings known when he commented that Alice, the second murder victim, had taken a bath in a house full of other lodgers but with the door unlocked. The bath Alice died in was also brought into court as an exhibit. The judge left the bench to follow the evidence that was given by Dr Billing, who explained how the woman died and used the bath to show clearly what he had seen and the findings of the medical evidence. He told the court that Alice's bathwater had been hot, and that in his opinion it was this that caused her to be "mazy" and suffering with "heart affectation", which in turn led to a faint which caused her death. John Hargreaves, an undertaker from Blackpool, then described to the court how Smith had visited him and said he wanted the funeral to be "as cheap as possible". Smith wanted a public grave, and for the funeral to take place as quickly as possible.

The second week of the trial began on 28th June 1915. It

reached its final stages a day later amidst "dramatic" outbursts from the accused. Marshall Hall didn't call for any evidence and Smith did not go into the witness box. As a result, Mr Bodkin gave his final address to the jury. Meanwhile, Smith was heard shouting at three detectives in turn as they gave evidence, calling them scoundrels and exclaiming: "I don't care two pence what you say, I've done no murder. I don't care if you sentence me to death." Dr Spilsbury told the court under cross-examination that death in the case of all three women was consistent with their legs having been lifted up and their heads submerged. Mr Bodkin told the jury that they had to "look unflinchingly at the evidence, but without any prejudice against the prisoner". He said: "You must start with the fact that the prisoner is a systematic bigamist ... He is married first in Leicester and there are also four other marriages proved relative to this inquiry."

At the end of June, Marshall Hall said: "Could any sane man have done what the prosecution allege against the prisoner? If Mr Bodkin's conclusions are sound it is one of the most diabolical crimes any records of any country have ever produced. You have to go back to the days of the Borgias, of systematic poisoning extending over a period of years." The public gallery was crowded as the judge told the jury that they would be given an opportunity to carefully examine the three baths. He also asked them to consider the possibility of Smith lifting his "wife" into the bath and holding her knees up, even though there was no evidence to support this. Mr Hall replied: "I submit that it is not open to the jury to consider any other hypothesis than that submitted by the Crown. I take a formal objection to your Lordship's alternative theory." The judge said that Mr Hall was entitled to his complaint, and that if the jury came up with a better theory than those suggested, they were quite at liberty to think it through.

In his speech for the defence, Mr Hall said that he could not say there was "an absence of motive", but told the jury that another judge in another case had said: "Motive is an important factor, but motive cannot convert suspicion into proof." In defending Smith, he asked if the "monster" that clearly carried out three murders could be the same man who had so tenderly looked after Miss Pegler, who had been "married" to the accused for seven years? "I say, with all the emphasis at my command, that if you will take the trouble to examine that bath and take the measurements of it and take the measurements of the body, it is a physical impossibility to have drowned the woman in that way under those conditions in eight inches of water."

The trial reached its dramatic conclusion in early July. When the guilty verdict was given in court, a murmur of intense relief ran round the room. George Smith was found guilty of the murder of Bessie Munday by drowning her in a bath. He looked pale, gripped the dock rail and glared angrily around the court. Until the last he had hoped he would be found not guilty. "You are telling the jury to hang me," was just one remark that he shouted to the judge from the dock. "This is a Christian country," he added in a mocking voice. Smith would leave the dock knowing he would be executed for his crime. It had taken the jury just 23 minutes to find him guilty. In his summing-up, the judge said there was no direct evidence that Smith murdered Bessie Munday or that he was present in the bathroom when she died. He continued: "If you convict him, you convict him on circumstantial evidence. I do not know that there is any certainty in the world. If any of you suffer from reading metaphysics you would probably be convinced that there is none." Meanwhile Smith continued his outbursts, saying: "You may go on for ever, but you will not make me into a murderer. I have done no murder. You would believe me here just as much as if I went into the witness box." The judge concluded: "In each of the cases the bathroom was unlocked; in two cases the women insured their lives within ten days of death; in each case two or three days before death the woman was taken to a strange doctor in a strange place where she was not known, complaining of a headache, and that doctor was the one called to the death. In each case the woman was found by the prisoner, and in each case he did not let the water out of the bath without permission. In each case there was a bigamous marriage, and in each case the burial was as cheap and obscure as possible. In each case he immediately went back to Miss Pegler."

Asked if he had anything to say about why he shouldn't suffer the death penalty, Smith looked blank for about 30 seconds before replying: "I am not guilty." Assuming the black cap, the judge said: "George Joseph Smith, the jury, after a careful and patient hearing, has found you guilty of the murder of Bessie

Munday. In doing so they must have taken an unfavourable view of your relations with Alice Burnham and Margaret Lofty. They have found you guilty of cold-blooded and heartless murder. In that verdict I entirely concur. Judges sometimes use this occasion to warn the public against the repetition of such crimes. They sometimes use the occasion to exhort the prisoner to repentance. I propose to take neither of those courses. I do not believe there is another man in England who needs to be warned against the commission of such a crime and to exhort you to repentance would be a waste of time." The judge, Mr Justice Scrutton, then passed the death sentence and ordered that the execution take place at Maidstone.

At the end of July 1915 Smith made an appeal, but it was dismissed by the Court of Criminal Appeal. At 8.00am on 13th August 1915, Smith was hanged at Maidstone jail. Although he had been resigned to his fate, he spent a restless night and received a visit from the chaplain, who remained with him until John Ellis, the executioner, entered his cell. Smith's arms were pinioned and he was walked with a warder on either side to the scaffold. His death was described as "instantaneous". Hundreds of people assembled outside the prison gates. Rumours circulated that Smith had confessed, but whether he did so was only known to the chaplain.

On the day Smith died, Caroline Thornhill took out a marriage licence and was married to Thomas Davies, from British Columbia.

# Confession of an Innocent Man

1915

A man who gave himself up for the murder of Alice Jarman, found dead in a ditch in Hyde Park in February 1915, was released after police inquiries found he had no connection to the crime. A verdict of wilful murder against person or persons unknown was returned at the Westminster inquest into the 40-year-old's death. At a previous hearing it was stated that the deceased's injuries could have been inflicted by a bayonet, and an old sword in a scabbard had been found by Westminster sewer workers in a Charlwood Street gully. The weapon was examined by Dr Trevor and Dr Wilcox from the Home Office, but there were no bloodstains on it or on its scabbard.

# Wilfred Hopper

1915

A sergeant in the 8th Welsh Reserve Battalion was sentenced to death by Mr Justice Atkin at Glamorgan Assizes on 9th March 1915. Wilfred Hopper had been found guilty of the murder of Private Enoch Daniel Dudley. He was recommended to mercy, and the judge announced that this would be forwarded to the "proper quarter". The evidence showed that after heavy drinking on Christmas Day 1914, a quarrel broke out when Dudley was accused by Hopper of stealing a bottle of whisky. Dudley and Private Lewis Gates were placed under arrest, and on the way to the drill hall Dudley was ordered to give up his bayonet. Hopper then fired at Private Dudley, killing him and seriously wounding Gates. The prisoner claimed that he had "brought his rifle down" in order to protect himself but had not intended to fire.

# Alfred Hemmings
## 1915

Alfred Hemmings was wanted by police in connection with the murder of Lilian Hubbard in Kennington in March 1915. At the Walworth inquest on 10th March into the 29-year-old widow's death, it was stated that she had been stabbed through the heart in a house in Aldred Street. Her brother-in-law, Thomas Moore, a bootmaker from Vauxhall, said that on the afternoon she died, a boy had brought him a pencilled note, saying it had been sent by a man "at the end of the street". The note read: "Your sister is murdered. Go to 66, Aldred Street, Kennington. You will find her there. She would not forgive, but she..."

Elizabeth Hemmings said the murdered woman was engaged to her son Alfred. She claimed that the couple regularly argued, and that two days before Lilian died, Hemmings had smashed all the furniture in her room. They had argued again on the morning that Lilian died, and he admitted to his mother that he had murdered his fiancé. He then disappeared. The jury returned a verdict of wilful murder against him.

# The Murder of Maggie Nally
## 1915

In January 1914, before the advent of the First World War, a small five-year-old boy was found dead under the seat in a carriage on the North London Railway. He was Willie Starchfield, son of John Starchfield, who was charged with the boy's murder. It was a strange case – shocking and callous – in which Starchfield maintained his innocence to the last. Willie, with his long golden curls, had often been mistaken for a girl. He had been sent out to run an errand for his mother, but never returned home.

In April 1915, London saw another "startling" murder case which had a number of similarities with the Starchfield case. The victim was a pretty little girl, aged seven, with round rosy cheeks, blue eyes and curly hair. Margaret Ellen Nally – known as Maggie – lived with her parents at 11 Amberley Road, Paddington. Her body, showing evidence of having been "mistreated", was discovered early on 5th April at Aldersgate Street station on the Metropolitan line. She was killed the day after her birthday after spending a "very happy" time visiting her aunt and grandfather and being allowed to buy sweets. It was thought that she had been enticed by a man who was masquerading as a woman. All night her parents searched for their daughter. When the little girl was eventually found she had been gagged and suffocated. Although police were thought to have had some clues, they didn't make any early arrests, but several fingerprints were taken from the room in which the body had been found.

Meanwhile, a family living near the Angel had been able to help police with their inquiries. Their daughter had been sent out from the family home in Duncan Terrace on Good Friday morning to buy a paper. She was stopped by a man who offered to take her to a picture palace. The child was frightened, but the man said: "Walk along to the tube station with me. I am meeting my sister there." He led her quickly towards the station, but when they got close, the girl escaped from him and ran home. The girl, aged 11, described the man as medium height, clean shaven, with a "fresh-coloured" complexion and dark hair. He was dressed in a black coat and dark trousers with a tweed cap.

The *Mirror* published the following description of the dead child: "Brown hair, tied with pink ribbon on the left side. Dressed in grey coat, with brown half-collar, two metal buttons and two side pockets. Also wearing white pinafore, with bright flowered sash. Dark red frock. Black button boots, with patent toes, nearly new. Black socks." Anyone who had seen the child was requested to communicate with Scotland Yard, and it was expected that an inquest would be opened on 7th April 1915 by Mr Walter Schroder, the Central London coroner.

The discovery of the tiny body was made after the last trains on the Metropolitan Line had run. Railway Inspector Groves was extinguishing the lights before closing the station when he noticed what appeared to be a bundle of clothing in a corner on the floor of the ladies' waiting room. Lifting the bundle, he was horrified to see it was the body of a child. As with Willie Starchfield, there were strangulation marks around the neck. A piece of torn material about a foot square found in the child's mouth had been used as a gag so that her screams wouldn't be heard, and more of this material was found nearby. Detectives were convinced that the murderer and his victim had arrived by train and did not enter the station from the street. They would have had to pass the ticket collector on duty in order to reach the waiting room, and it was felt that he would have definitely seen them late at night on a Sunday when there were few people about, although at this time there were fewer staff on duty. The police were also convinced that the child had been strangled where she was found; that the murderer knew the ladies' waiting room attendant finished at 7.00pm on a Sunday night, and so deliberately chose the station for his crime.

Exhaustive inquiries got underway as soon as the grim story came to light. The *Mirror* pointed to the conclusion that the girl had been decoyed near her home off the Edgware Road and that she and the murderer had joined the Metropolitan Line near there some time after 8 o'clock that Sunday night. She had left her aunt's house at about that time with Alice Scott (5), who was her friend, to buy sweets. Just a few minutes later Alice reappeared, saying that Maggie had gone home. Mrs Nally said: "Maggie was the dearest little kiddie God ever put breath into. She had bright blue eyes and brown, curly hair. I cannot understand how anyone could have enticed her away, because I had always warned her about following or going with strange men, and I am sure she would do what I had told her to." Mr Nally said: "Maggie went over to Marylebone, which is quite close to us, to her grandfather on Sunday evening. She was last seen playing about in Carlisle Street at a quarter past eight. Since that time she was not seen by anyone until they found her at Aldersgate Street. We were searching nearly all the night for her."

On 7th April, a bus conductor told the *Mirror* that he had seen the little girl before she was murdered. He said that a man had got on his bus at Chapel Street, Edgware Road between 8.15pm and 8.20pm. The man's clothing looked "rough and dirty". He was accompanied by a girl aged between seven and eight, who had a healthy appearance although she was crying. The conductor went on: "I noticed the man was under the influence of drink. The child appeared to be timid of the man, as if she did not want to go with him. On the platform the child stood hesitating … The man got hold of her sleeve and said: 'Up you go,' and followed her up the stairs.

"When I got on the top I approached the man with the child

and asked for the fares. He took no notice and was holding his head down as if he was dozing. I stood looking at the man for some time. He did not seem to observe me standing there, and while I was taking stock of him he turned his head towards the child and told her to 'shut up.' I then said to the man: 'Has she lost her hat?' and he answered in a snappish manner: 'Oh, I don't know!' I then took a bag of dried figs out of my pocket and offered them to the child. She did not make any attempt to take any so I took out a large one and gave it to her.

"On our arrival at King's Cross they did not alight until the omnibus pulled up at the corner of Gray's Inn Road, when the man and child descended the stairs and stepped on to the footway. When on the footway the man got hold of the girl's sleeve and led her to a whelk-stall just outside the station. I did not see them have anything."

Superintendent Ottaway told the *Mirror* that the conductor had seen the body of Maggie Nally in the mortuary and identified it as that of the little girl whom he had seen on his bus. He was certain that he had seen Maggie.

Another statement that was of great interest to the police was made by a guard. He said: "On April 4 I was in charge of a train which left Hammersmith at 9.19pm for Aldersgate. The train arrived at Aldersgate Station at 9.45pm. A woman and a little girl got out of the carriage. The woman was about thirty-two to thirty-five years of age ... She appeared to be of the working class. The child had no hat on. Her hair was wavy and there was a bow of light-coloured ribbon on the side of her head rather towards the back. She had a coat on and something white showed below it like a pinafore. As my carriage left the station I saw the girl and the woman walking towards the way out, which is also the direction for the women's waiting room."

The police hoped that if the statements were seen by the man and woman involved, and they had a genuine explanation, then they could be ruled out of enquiries. Obviously, neither of the statements fitted the circumstances exactly, but if the girl had a fig in her stomach it would go a long way towards establishing if the conductor's sighting was that of Maggie. The *Mirror* wrote: "In support of the conductor's statement it has been suggested that the murderer might have been a soldier on leave from the front [the man had been wearing a soldier's overcoat] who had become demented owing to the strain of the life in the trenches. It was also suggested that the child's hat was blown away by the wind and lost, thus causing her to cry and giving the murderer an opportunity of making friends with her."

Dr Waldo, the city coroner, opened the inquest on 9th April 1915 by briefly reviewing the facts of the tragedy. He said: "It appears on the face of it to have been an atrocious and cruel murder." It was clear when she gave evidence that Maggie's mother was heartbroken. Alice, who was the last person to see Maggie other than her murderer, also went into the witness box and was questioned by her mother, Betsy, at the coroner's suggestion. The inquest was adjourned until 22nd April.

John Henry Nally, Maggie's father, was the first witness after adjournment. He described how he and his wife had searched for their daughter when she didn't come home. She had been wearing a hat when he had last seen her. The child's clothes were produced and identified by her father; Mrs Nally could barely contain her grief as the small items were held up. The piece of material that had been found in the child's mouth was identified by Mrs Nally, who said she had given it to her as a hankie. Betsy Scott said that she had been feeling unwell on the Sunday night and had given Alice and Maggie 1*d* to go and buy some sweets. Mr Groves then described finding Maggie. He said: "The child was lying on its back with its feet towards the door and its little arms outstretched, the back of the hand being on the floor. The right cheek was towards the floor. The mouth was open and there was something discoloured in it. I formed the opinion at once that the child had been murdered – suffocated."

Superintendent Ottaway gave some further facts, and Dr James Kearney said he was called to the station at midnight and saw the child, who was being given artificial respiration. Dr Spilsbury said he had made a post-mortem examination and found evidence of two separate meals. He concluded that the cause of death was asphyxia due to a foreign body in the mouth followed by syncope due to the condition "of status lymphaticus".

At the funeral of Maggie Nally on 26th April 1915, the coffin was borne from her house to the hearse and from the church to the grave by four corporals of the Army Service Corps. "They came", said Corporal Griffin, a relative of the family, "to show the sympathy of the ASC and the resentment of the Army at the slur which had been cast upon them by the allegation that a soldier had been responsible for the crime." During the First World War, soldiers were not seen as heroes as they often are today, and the general public showed little sympathy for the conditions they faced. When confronted by the possibility that a soldier was responsible for the death of a child, public resentment was fuelled by a media frenzy which escalated the situation. Messages came for Maggie's family from soldiers at the front. A private in the Northumberland Fusiliers, who was wounded in Belgium, sent a pencil sketch of the little girl, while a corporal enclosed some money for a wreath. Meanwhile, in Dover a soldier gave himself up as the murderer, telling an attendant at a picture palace that he had committed the crime. However, police discredited his story because he was drunk. (It was later proved that he hadn't even been in London at the time.) It turned out that he had admitted to murdering another little girl some time before, which also wasn't true. He was handed over to the military authorities to be dealt with for "breaking out of barracks".

Police were still hopeful of finding Maggie's hat. In the hunt for it they discovered a ticket at Baker Street station on which the words "I intend to kill a girl tonight" had been written. It didn't provide much of a clue. However, by now they knew that Maggie had eaten a substantial meal within an hour and a half of her death, and they were anxious to find the restaurant where the murderer had taken her.

At the inquest into the child's death, a verdict of wilful murder by person or persons unknown was returned by the coroner's jury. What the *Mirror* didn't report was that Maggie Nally had been seriously sexually assaulted. Although a man was reported to have been hanging around tube stations offering little girls sweets he was never apprehended, and the perpetrator of Maggie's murder was never caught.

# Alice Mary Wheatley
## 1915

An 11-year-old girl stood in the witness box next to her seven-year-old sister, who had to stand on a stool, to give evidence at the coroner's inquiry into the death of their mother. Annie Wootten, wife of Lieutenant Albert Wootten from the 10th Bedfordshire Regiment, was found dead at her home in Rotherfield Street, Islington, London. At first witnesses thought Annie had died from a fall, but later a bullet wound was found. A young barmaid known as Marie Lanteri was reported to have committed the murder, and was held on remand.

Lily Wootten told the inquiry that after her mother put her to bed she heard "a footstep in the passage". She then heard her mother talking to another person, but the two voices were not loud and there were no angry exchanges. The child said that her mother later went to the kitchen, and she saw her go outside with a glass of water. She then returned upstairs. Lily asked: "Mother, who is it?" and Annie replied: "Mrs Higson's friend." The girl then heard the voices again, and "two bangs". The coroner said: "What were the bangs like?" and the child replied: "Like the side room door slamming." Lily heard her mother cry out: "Oh! Oh!" after each bang and said: "I then heard someone go away and the front door was closed. My mother then called out: 'Lily, Lily' and Ivy and I rushed out of bed and found mother sitting on the edge of the top of the stairs. We tried to pull her back but she fell down the stairs." Ivy told the inquiry that on the night her mother died she had heard a strange voice in the passage saying: "Give me some water, I am thin and hungry." Ivy also heard the stranger demanding money: "I heard mother say: 'Oh, don't. I have got four children …'" She then heard the other woman say: "Oh, I would not for the world."

Cora Higson told the inquiry that she visited Mrs Wootten three times a week. She confirmed that she only had one friend in London, whom she referred to as Marie Wheatley. She had seen a woman standing against the railings of Annie's house with her back to them; the woman looked like Marie Wheatley, but she couldn't be sure. It was understood by the Woottens and Cora Higson that Wheatley was to be known as "Mrs Higson's friend". Asked why this was the case, Mrs Higson said: "I suppose because Mr Wootten must have been carrying on with her and Mrs Wootten did not want her family to know who she was."

On 9th April 1915, Marie Lanteri, otherwise known as Wheatley, was charged at the North London police court with murder; the accused had not attended the inquest the day before. James Jordon, a sorter, told how he was called to the Woottens' house and found Mrs Wootten lying head downwards. Her little girl was standing by her side, looking down at her. He said there was a hole in Mrs Wootten's blouse that was smouldering, but he didn't see anyone else in the house or any firearms.

Frederick Dixon also saw Mrs Wootten lying on the floor. He had been in the area because he had previously lived at 114 Rotherfield Street, and thought that a telegram his wife told him about was for him. The telegram did not spell his name correctly and no one knew where it had come from, but Lieutenant Wootten had read it out. It said: "There has been murder here." Lily then told both men that a woman had visited the house who was Mrs Higson's friend.

The inquiry heard that Mrs Wootten had previously asked Wheatley: "Don't you think you are doing very wrong by taking a man from his wife and children?" Giving evidence on 12th April, Lieutenant Wootten was interrupted by Wheatley, who exclaimed: "Oh, you lie!" But, Lieutenant Wootten said that Wheatley had replied "Yes" and expressed her love for him when she had been asked the question. He also alleged that Wheatley had asked him several times to take his children and leave his wife, but he had told her it was impossible. The coroner asked the cheating husband if Wheatley had ever made threats to his late wife, to which he replied that she had said: "If ever I meet your wife I am sure I will do her in." Wootten also said that Wheatley had told him that her father had a revolver. He told the coroner that Wheatley had shown him a cardboard target which she said she had shot with a Morris tube rifle, the results of which showed "excellent shooting". He also stated that the accused had said: "I can't bear the thought of your being married and belonging to another woman; you are mine!" The witness then identified an anonymous letter which he had received towards the end of March 1915, which read: "Waiting to hear that your services are no longer required. I see you are going to get off. Your kiddies come next. Sure as your name is B. Wootten I will do you in. You asked me once to do a dirty trick for you. Now it's my turn. You passed me as if I was dirt. I don't forget."

Wootten told Mr Pratt – counsel for the defence – that when he first got to know Wheatley he didn't tell her he was married, but she soon found out. He told the inquest he had never promised to marry his lover, or led her to think that he would. Mr Pratt said: "So she would gain nothing by your wife's death?" Wootten replied: "No." He said that he had met Wheatley in October 1914, when she was employed as a barmaid at the George Hotel, and later introduced her to his wife Annie. He told the inquest that after his wife's death he had confronted his lover, but she had denied that she had been to the house and certainly hadn't confessed to murder. Wootten admitted that he had agreed to provide for Wheatley until she "got a situation". He had seen her on the day of the murder, and she had told him she had been unsuccessful in finding a situation, remarking: "I am a great drain on you." She told him that she would give anybody £5 if they would shoot her. Wootten told her "not to be silly" and that something would turn up. He later received the message that something had happened to his wife.

George Higson said that he had written a letter for Annie to copy in response to a letter from Wheatley that had declared her feelings for Bert Wootten, which was when Mrs Wootten had discovered he was having an affair. She had asked her husband's lover to stay away from him and told her that until he had met her he had been a devoted family man. Higson said that in February 1915 Wootten and Wheatley agreed to stay away from each other for the sake of his wife and children.

On 4th May 1915, as Wootten gave evidence in the continuing inquest, Wheatley made copious notes when she wasn't staring at her former lover. The *Mirror* stated: "Few men have had to make such painful revelations in such tragic circumstances as Lieutenant Wootten ..." He told the inquest that his wife had discovered he was having an affair and that "she had a rival", and that he had decided not to continue to see Wheatley. He also said that the barmaid had constantly asked him to leave his wife, but that he had refused. Wootten described the moment he had had to look at his dead wife's face. As the *Mirror* wrote: "It was a very moving story of one man and two women with a grim background of tragedy."

At the start of Wheatley's trial in June at the Old Bailey, the court heard that when Annie had asked the accused to stay away from her family, Wheatley had replied: "I can't help it. I love Bert." Counsel said that after Wheatley had lost her job as a barmaid in Shoreham, Wootten had taken her into his billet, claiming she was his wife. According to Wheatley, she didn't learn he was married until he brought her to London. She later moved to Ecclesbourne Road, literally around the corner from Annie Wootten. Counsel for the prosecution said that this gave her the chance to murder her love rival. Wheatley pleaded not guilty to wilful murder.

The following day, 22nd June, Bert Wootten was the chief witness at the Old Bailey. He repeated the evidence he had given at the inquest. Mr Higson was next in the witness box, followed by Lily Wootten. The court then heard that a revolver and cartridges had been found in an attaché case at the accused's address. A domestic servant, Violet Thorn, who had seen the revolver wrapped in a nightdress, while working for Mrs Allen who owned the house where Wheatley had a room, was called to give evidence, but Detective Sergeant Wesley said that when the accused was arrested she denied having a revolver.

The jury took just 12 minutes, on 28th June 1915, to find Wheatley not guilty. When the verdict was announced there was subdued applause. The judge ordered that Wheatley be discharged. Her counsel had warned the jury of convicting her on purely circumstantial evidence, and said she had been "tricked and betrayed, cast aside and accused of murder by Lieutenant Wootten". In his summing up Mr Justice Lush said: "It is difficult to speak temperately at the conduct of Lieutenant Wootten towards his wife and towards the accused.

"Wootten comes before you as a discredited witness, and had this case rested upon his evidence alone I should have had no hesitation in telling you that you would do wrong in acting upon it and convicting this woman. I do not only speak of the infidelity to his wife. That is bad enough and has no doubt given and will no doubt give him cause for reflection and shame as long as he lives ... It seems to me shocking that when he was living with the accused as man and wife he should, whether it was dictated to him by the prisoner, or not, have written to the parents of this girl, 'Dear Dad and Mother,' in order to deceive them into thinking that he was married to their daughter and to no one else." However, the judge did not suggest that Wootten had murdered his wife.

# Ada Ann Elms

1915

"Mother charged with murder," read the headlines in the *Mirror* on 17th December 1915. Accompanying the dramatic story was a photograph of the accused woman, taken with her four children the day before tragedy struck. In the picture were Ada Ann Elms,

Elizabeth (9), Thomas (6), Alfred (3) and 18-month-old William. Elms was charged at Brentford police station with four murders and with attempting suicide.

The 32-year-old woman had cut her own throat at the family home in Colne Road, Twickenham, London. The four children were found dead in a bed on the first floor of the property. Detective Inspector Wright said he had seen letters written by the woman confessing that she had drowned the children. When the children were discovered, partially covered by the bedclothes, their "heads were tied up ready for burial". A doll had been placed in the arms of the little girl and a teddy bear between her and Thomas. When told that her children had been found, Elms said: "Are they dead? They have not brought them back to life again have they?" When the reply came that they hadn't, she said: "Thank God, he has taken them to his rest."

The inquest in Twickenham on the bodies of the four children began on 20th December. As Elms' letters were read out she wept bitterly. The jury returned a verdict of wilful murder after hearing from a letter she wrote to her husband: "I am taking my little children with me, as I would not have them to fight through this hard world as I have had to do. I have always tried to do my best for my children. I have had seven and lost three. Don't call me a woman, but I will stick to them in death. I do not care what becomes of me. If I do not have the pluck to kill myself I will suffer my doom on the scaffold. I cannot live in misery and see my children go down in the gutter."

In another letter she wrote: "Dear Tom, I drowned the children at six o'clock till seven p.m., and waited to see if they were dead. This is two o'clock. I am trying to do myself in. If I do not succeed I must suffer the gallows."

Elms was committed for trial at the Central Criminal Court by Brentford magistrates on 23rd December for drowning her four children in the copper. The prisoner said she would not call any witnesses, adding: "I did it. I left home with the intention of giving myself up and I gave myself up." She was found guilty and insane at the Old Bailey and sentenced to be detained at His Majesty's Pleasure.

# Welsh Hill Murder
## 1916

Guilty but insane was the verdict of the jury on 30th October 1916 at the Carmarthen Assizes trial of David Davies for the murder of Dr Glyn Jones. Davies, of Blaenrbysglog Farm, shot the doctor at his parents' home. Jane Davies said she had heard a gunshot while in her bedroom tending to her ill husband. When she went outside, she had seen her son and the doctor struggling with a gun. The gun fired. She had heard Davies say: "Just shot you," and said to the court that his "mind was very bad at times".

After a five-day search in the mountains the accused was captured by police. Davies had been hiding out amongst some rocks, and was pounced on by officers as he brandished a carving knife. After being handcuffed, he stated to police officers that his father was better and he didn't want the doctor to visit him. "There are plenty of vagabonds going about the country poisoning people," he added. "I hardly knew for a moment what had happened," he said later, "as he still clung to me and having the gun in my hand I used it. I struck out blindly."

In court, a police witness said the accused had asked officers if they had revolvers. When he discovered that they hadn't, he said: "If I had seen you coming towards me in time one of you would have gone, and you could not blame me for doing it. I had sharpened the knife for the purpose. Seeing somebody after me, I should have made for the blue. I only wanted three-penny-worth to finish both of you."

After the six-hour trial Mr Justice Lush said the prisoner would be detained "during His Majesty's pleasure".

# Trench Tragedy
## 1917

The body of Lieutenant and Quartermaster Watterton, RAMC, was found in a disused trench. Sergeant O'Donnell, RAMC, remanded in custody on suspicion in connection with the tragedy, wasn't present as evidence was given at the adjourned inquest in Aldershot on 12th January 1917. The jury returned a verdict of wilful murder against Sergeant O'Donnell, and he was committed by the coroner to Winchester jail. Giving evidence, Sergeant Ney said that a broken brush handle had been found near the body, and the head a few feet away. The dead man's watch had stopped at nine o'clock. There were 21 wounds on his head – none of which were self-inflicted. Watterton's daughter had seen him at about 8.00pm on the night he died with O'Donnell, who regularly visited the family home. He had already asked Watterton if he could marry his daughter, but the proposal had been declined on his daughter's behalf. When O'Donnell revisited the house on the night Watterton died, at around 11.30pm, he asked the man's daughter if she had seen a "truncheon" he had left there earlier that evening. He was describing the brush – with the bristles removed – that was found near the victim. Sergeant Lee George O'Donnell was charged with wilful murder on 16th January 1917.

Giving evidence at the hearing, Watterton's daughter didn't glance at O'Donnell at all, while he constantly stared and smiled at her. Mr Pearce, prosecuting, told how a truncheon found near the dead man was similar to the one known to have been in O'Donnell's possession. Watterton was known to have been killed between 8.00pm and 9.00pm, at a time when O'Donnell could not account for his movements. He was alleged to have told police when he was arrested that he couldn't hurt anyone because "I am a conscientious objector", which was why he joined his corps. Four £1 notes, found on the accused at the time, were sent to the Home Office analyst John Webster, who found traces of blood on each one. On 18th January, O'Donnell reserved his defence at the resumed hearing and was committed for trial.

Meanwhile, Private Hislop, RAMC, a telephone operator at the Isolation Hospital, said he had seen O'Donnell try Lieutenant Watterton's office door at about midnight on 1st January. He had stayed for about 45 minutes, although the key wasn't found in its usual place. O'Donnell had told witnesses that he had work to do for Watterton, but QMS Willis, RAMC, told the hearing that the safe in Watterton's office was kept locked and that the dead man carried the key at all times. This key was still missing on 2nd January, although it was eventually found by a council worker outside the police station. The safe was known to house a large amount of money that Canadian patients had brought to the hospital. Responsibility for the money had worried Watterton, and he had said as much in front of both his daughter and O'Donnell on more than one occasion.

O'Donnell was said to have written some letters to Miss Watterton, and these were read before Mr Justice Darling at the Hants Assizes on 9th February 1917, on day one of the trial. Prosecuting, Clavell Salter said that Watterton had been murdered by the "brush" that had been in O'Donnell's possession. The two men had been together on the night of the murder. Mr Salter also told the court that O'Donnell had written to Sergeant Hesketh, and stated that the accused had said: "Now, Hesketh, for God's sake clear up these two hours for me. Say you saw me at a social

Home Front Killers

or anywhere." To bandsman Izood he wrote: "Help me clear up the two hours. Say you spoke to me about a quarter to nine in D block. I will give you £10 when I come out." A friend named Finch was alleged to have been offered £250 if he would tell police that O'Donnell had been drunk and that he put him into bed. A letter to Finch said: "This is my last hope." Superintendent Davis told the court that when asked to account for the two hours he was "missing", O'Donnell said he was at a "social" at the training school where he sang a song, but Sergeant Hesketh had been at the social and hadn't seen the accused. The trial continued.

Sergeant O'Donnell was found guilty of murder and sentenced to death. He was hanged at Winchester jail on 29th March 1917.

# Frederick Charles Livingstone

1917

Southend police court charged Frederick Charles Livingstone, aged just 16, with the murder of Louisa Burrows Walker on 19th February 1917. He was accused of shooting her with a revolver in Eastwood. Police Constable Geddy stated that at 6.45am he met Livingstone in London Road, Hadleigh, where he handcuffed the accused and searched him. When cautioned, the youth said: "I have not got the revolver, I threw it away." They were accompanied along London Road by Police Constable Reeve, who told the court that the accused said: "I brought the revolver from St Albans with me." The officer added that Livingstone was then cautioned again, but he stated: "I shot the woman for money. I wanted money." On the application of the Chief Constable, eight days' remand was granted.

At the end of the police court proceedings Livingstone was taken by car to Leigh, where the coroner's inquest was taking place. Eleanor Walker, the sister of the dead woman, told the inquest that Louisa had left home between one and two o'clock on the day she died to go shopping in Leigh. She took a small black handbag. After PC Geddy repeated his evidence, the jury returned a wilful murder verdict, and Livingstone was committed for trial on the coroner's warrant.

"Death Sentence On Boy" read the headline in the *Mirror* on 9th June 1917. The day before, at the Essex Assizes in Chelmsford, Livingstone had been sentenced to death for the murder of Louisa. The jury had recommended mercy on account of his age, which was supported by the judge. Livingstone was reported to have claimed that watching men shooting people for money at the cinema gave him the idea, but said he knew it was wrong. He was granted a reprieve on 26th June.

# The Murder of Janet "Janey" Oven

## 1917

On 18th May 1917 London solicitor Mr T. Davidson was driving to the station with his wife, in Bricket Wood, near Watford, when he noticed someone dragging a body towards the side of the road up ahead. The man disappeared almost immediately, but Mr Davidson thought he was "rough-looking" and that he wore a brown cloth cap. He stopped his car, and saw straightaway that the woman was dead. She had been shot in the neck.

The body was later identified as Janet "Janey" Oven, a single woman aged 26 who lived with her parents a mile and a half outside Bricket Wood. Before this, Janet had lived in Hull for two years. On the morning she died, she had been on her way to the station to catch a train to work: she was a draper's assistant in Watford. No one could work out why the pretty young woman had been killed in a Hertfordshire wood. "What was the underlying motive for a most dramatic and mysterious crime?" asked the *Mirror*. Three days after the murder, despite the fact that "a small army of detectives" was engaged on the case, "the assailant" was still "at large".

Five minutes before Janet passed along the wooded lane where she was killed, a cottager's wife saw a man walking in the direction of Bricket Wood station. He was regarded as a stranger in the area, but the witness had seen him on three other mornings in the week Janet died. Since her murder, the man had vanished. The police attached considerable importance to this, and circulated the following description of the man: "Age about 30; height about 5ft. 8in.; full face; dressed in dark brown overcoat, light trousers (rather loose in the legs), cloth cap; of respectable appearance." Beyond this description, the man remained a mystery. Meanwhile, it was reported that Janet's handbag was missing. The police had nothing more to go on.

For three weeks – morning and evening – Janet Oven had walked the mile and a half from her parents' house to Bricket Wood station and back home again. She took the train to Watford, where she worked at Messrs Cundell's drapers. She was well liked, quiet and modest, and not known to have a "sweetheart". Janet had been in "good spirits" as she waved goodbye to her mother and hurried off to the station.

By this time, it had been reported that Mr Davidson had not heard a shot before he saw Janet being dragged across the road. Dropping his burden into a "brush-covered dip", the man had disappeared into the wood. Janet was killed instantaneously. If the motive was robbery, why did the killer leave the young woman's jewellery behind? Why did he only take her small bag, which contained nothing more than a few letters and a piece of cream-coloured cloth? Her purse – containing just 5d – was left untouched. The police had to consider that robbery was not the motive for the crime.

Home Front Killers

On day four of the murder hunt, the police were still no closer to finding the killer. They were actively pursuing every lead they could, but the clues were described as "flimsy" at best. The revolver, believed to be of heavy calibre, still hadn't been found either.

On 24th May 1917 a verdict of wilful murder against "some person unknown" was returned at Janet Oven's inquest. John Knight Oven, Janet's father, said that his daughter had been tired of lodgings and had wanted to "come home to her mother". She hadn't mentioned anything that had happened in Hull that might have encouraged her to return home. As far as he was aware she only had female friends in Hull; there were no known male friends. Mr Davidson, who admitted that he was rather deaf in one ear, said his wife had heard a shot as they set off from their home towards the station. Susan Powell had also heard a shot, about five minutes after Janet had passed her in the lane – the young woman had been walking alone. Dr Leslie Bates, the police surgeon, said that at the post-mortem he had found a bullet wound in Janet's right temple. A bullet was found near the wound. There was also a small bullet wound near the lobe of the left ear, but the bullet from this hadn't been recovered.

On 6th July 1917, Albert Edward Lorford (16), a labourer from Wood Green, found himself in the dock in St Albans, charged on remand with the murder of Janet Oven. He was described as having a "vacant" expression. On 13th July, St Albans police court heard the counsel for the prosecution state that Lorford had confessed to the murder. Mr F.J. Sims, Assistant Director of Public Prosecutions, said that on 28th June, Lorford had made his confession to the governor of the Borstal Institution at Rochester where he had been committed for an offence since the beginning of June 1917. Lorford said: "On 26 December I absconded from Red Hill Farm School. I lived at Watford from January until May. I left Watford in the beginning of May and went to Brighton. I stole one revolver and twenty-three cartridges from the military rifle range in the Lower Esplanade owned by Miss Grant. I walked back to Watford and on arriving there I had no money or food. Next morning I was walking along the Watford and St Albans main road, and I saw Miss J. Oven coming along. I went up the Bricket Wood-lane, and when she came up I asked her for some money. I held the pistol up and she tried to snatch at it, and the trigger went off."

Lorford was committed for trial at Hertfordshire Assizes. The case was extremely similar to that of Frederick Livingstone (also 16), who had been found guilty of the murder of Louisa Burrows Walker earlier that same year. The motive – money – was also the same. In the witness box Lorford, who appeared cool and collected, said he was walking along the road with a loaded revolver in his pocket when he saw Janet Oven. "Not having a penny," he said, "I demanded money and put up the revolver. She snatched at it. I tried to pull it back and the revolver went off. She fell flat on her face. I had no intention of injuring her. I confessed to the Governor because I saw in the papers that another man was likely to be arrested." Lorford received seven years' penal servitude after he was convicted of manslaughter on 20th November 1917. Mr Justice Bray told him that had he been older he would have received double the sentence.

# Douglas Malcolm
1917

Douglas Malcolm (34), a lieutenant in the Royal Artillery stationed at Headquarters in France, was remanded at Marylebone police court on 14th August 1917 on a charge of murdering Count Anton Baumberg. He had shot the victim in a boarding house in Porchester Place, Hyde Park, London.

The accused, who was in mufti, was understood to be a member of the Bath Club. Mr Baumberg was described by police as a "Russian Pole". Detective McHattie said there were "apparently four bullet wounds" in the victim's body – one in the centre of the forehead, one on the left side of the windpipe, one in the front of the chest and one on the left side of the chest. The victim's mouth was open and his lips were swollen, as if he had been dealt a fierce blow. He also had blood over his face, chest and hands. When charged, the accused said: "Very well, charge me with what you like," and when the charge was read to him he added: "Very well, I did it for my honour."

More disclosures followed at the inquest on 20th August. The court heard that Malcolm had entered the count's bedroom, having told him he was a detective. After his murder, Baumberg was revealed to have used a number of different names, and claimed to be a Russian subject. It was alleged that he had lived on intimate terms with Lieutenant Malcolm's wife while the Royal Artillery officer was away on active service at the Front. This was the motive for the victim's murder. Mrs Malcolm was described as "a most attractive, handsome woman" who moved in "high social circles" and was "highly connected". By arrangement with the Public Prosecutor, Mr Bingley, the magistrate at Marylebone police court decided not to proceed with the charge against Lieutenant Malcolm for the wilful murder of Baumberg for a further week.

"Justifiable homicide in self-defence" was the verdict of the Paddington coroner's jury, in what was described by the *Mirror* as "one of the most sensational love dramas – the Malcolm case – ever told at a London inquest".

When asked to tell the jury how she felt about "Count de Borch," known as Anton Baumberg, Mrs Malcolm said: "I loved this man." The count was known now to have received 10 bullet wounds, but he remained a man of mystery. The inquiry, conducted by Major Dunlop, said that he believed the victim was the son of a man named Borch, and his mother had later married a man named Baumberg. The victim had admitted to living with "Baroness Baumberg" at some point during his earlier life. It was thought that the baroness might have been a spy, but the count was said to have had no knowledge of that. However, at the police court, Malcolm said that Baumberg was "a white slave trafficker and a spy. Scotland Yard know all about him." He told the magistrate: "I see there are wicked and scurrilous reports about my wife having had intimate relations with this man. I swear it is absolutely false – absolutely false." In her letters to the victim, Mrs Malcolm addressed him as "Wolfheart" and "Wolf", and signed herself "Squee". Among the letters read out in court was one from Malcolm to Baumberg, challenging him to a duel in France. There was also a letter from Malcolm to his wife, in which he thanked God for "having sent me over in time to save you from this devil incarnate. Your honour is saved." Reading this letter, the coroner's voice showed great emotion.

Mrs Malcolm told the inquest that she had met Baumberg on 1st April at a tea party, and he had asked permission to call on her. He called frequently after this, and told her that he had no real title because de Borch was his birth father. He also told Mrs Malcolm that his passport was with his luggage at a German station and he had no way of retrieving it. He said he had been in Berlin at the outbreak of war and had had to leave quickly. He feared being shot as an English spy. Mrs Malcolm had written: "Dear Count – My husband has returned, and so I shall not be in to-night. I will let you know when I shall be able to see you again, but I fear not for some time – Yours sincerely." Mrs Malcolm told the court that she had met Baumberg at her flat in Cadogan Square, London, as well as at other places, including a friend's house in a village in Hampshire, where they had both been invited as guests. They had travelled there with another woman friend. When asked by the coroner if she knew her husband was home on leave she replied: "No, it was about twelve o'clock midday and I was upstairs in the count's bedroom." Confirming she was with the count at the time, she said: "I heard my husband call from the hallway up the stairs. He pushed the door wide open and came in. There was a frightful scene, as my husband objected to the count." The coroner asked if her husband said very much and she continued: "He did not say much, but struck [the] deceased with his fists on his forehead." She confirmed that the victim had not fought back, but fell down before putting his head down and raising his hands to ward off the blows. He then fainted. Asked if her husband did anything after that, Mrs Malcolm said she didn't know, and that Mrs Brett had arrived soon after.

The accused's wife also admitted that she had mentioned the victim a number of times in letters to her husband – describing him as "an ordinary friend" – and said she hadn't made any disclosures to her husband. She had implored her husband to divorce her when she told him that she had been having an intimate relationship with Baumberg. However, Malcolm refused to countenance this, and had "vehemently and fervently" tried to persuade her to give up the victim. The coroner then read a letter from Malcolm to Baumberg: "You refused to fight all right I challenge you to a duel – pistols or swords, you can take your choice. Tell me where you want to meet me as soon as possible.

Home Front Killers

Seconds will be a difficulty to me, but I will get one.-Douglas Malcolm." Mrs Malcolm said she had told her husband that she would try to give up the victim. She wrote to Baumberg: "Wolfheart, I have just a few moments to write. I was so happy to receive your letter and to know that you are well, and, of course, hearing from you comforts me a little. D. has written you, and if the dreadful affair comes off I think I shall die. Wolf, write to me and seal your letter to Piper [the maid] and give my love to Bunny and tell her I have not a moment as D. never leaves me or I would write her. I am so sorry to have let her in for a horrible scene … I am half-dazed – I cannot write all that is in my heart – my love to my Wolf [Signed] Squee." Another letter from Malcolm to Baumberg was also read: "Count Anthony de Borch, I have had no reply to my challenge and, in case you have not received the note written on New Milton Station I sent you by post from there, I again challenge you, and leave the choice of weapons to you. You will see it is better that this should happen in France. Therefore, I earnestly hope you will arrange to get to France as early as possible." Mrs Malcolm wrote again to Baumberg: "Wolf, D. has gone to the War Office to try and get an extension of leave, and so I am alone and able to write to you. I am thinking of you always. Let me know all your news. He has written to you again about this wretched duel. What are you going to do about it? It is awful, this uncertainty. Where are you coming up to town I hope soon, as I do not like you being alone with anyone. Is it horrid of me? I have had to promise not to see you till the war is over. For my mother's sake I do it. Wolf, I hope you are not suffering as much as I am. Oh, I do so hope you are not. My heart is breaking, so I cannot write sense or what I feel. Will this suffering never end?"

Mrs Malcolm said that when her husband was away again she wrote to him, explaining clearly that she had seen Baumberg several times after he had gone. She said she didn't want to give her husband of three years false hope. When Malcolm returned home there was a "scene", during which Mrs Malcolm said she absolutely could not stay with her husband. "I mentioned that it was contemplated that I should go with him [Baumberg] on the continent ... Mr Malcolm visited Scotland Yard and came back and said that he had found that deceased was a procurer. I said that I could not live with my husband all the same." When asked why, Mrs Malcolm said because she was in love with Baumberg. In another letter, Malcolm stated: "To Count de Borch, If I ever hear of you trying to steal or even talk to my wife again, wherever I am I will get leave and hunt you out and give you such a thrashing that even your own mother will not know you again. I will thrash you until I have maimed you for life. This I swear before God, in whom I believe and who is my witness. D. Malcolm." The coroner then read another letter from Malcolm (who had said that in the event of his death all his money would be left to his mother) to his wife: "My dear very own darling Dorothy, Dear God, there is a time for everything. Everything points to it that this creature is the most unutterable blackguard ever born. I shudder to think of it, that he ever does even speak to you drives me mad. I simply cannot stand it any longer. I am going to thrash him until he is unrecognizable. I may shoot him if he has got a gun. I expect he has, as he is too much of a coward to stand a thrashing. If the inevitable has got to happen, of course, I may get it in the neck first. You see I am quite cool. If that happens, oh, believe me, my own little darling, my beloved soul, whom I love so absolutely, believe me, it is for you only.

"I swear to you that I love you more than any man has ever loved a woman before, and if there is any wrong in me it is because I love you too much. You are a brave woman. You are noble, honourable and upright, with what a beautiful soul … Good-bye, which means God be with you. I love you, and I shall go on loving you for eternity, for ever and ever. I know I shall meet you in the next world if the worst happens, when you will come to me with open arms, and those beautiful eyes, shining and say to me, 'Douggie, I forgive.'"

When Mr Roome, representing Malcolm, asked the accused's wife if she knew Baumberg had deceived her, she replied that she didn't.

After his arrest Malcolm had said: "Ah, well, it is all over now. I went to give him a good thrashing with the whip. I gave him one before but he is such a cad. I have done all I can to keep him away from my wife and her from him … You can imagine how I felt when I saw the cad who was trying to get my wife to go away with him and me in France helpless to defend her honour. Can you wonder at what I did in the impulse of the moment, when I saw the cur before me who was luring my wife to dishonour?" Mr Roome cited that the provocation in the case should reduce the murder charge to manslaughter, and the jury returned a verdict of justifiable homicide in self-defence.

A woman shorthand writer who attended an inquiry into Baumberg confirmed that the mystery man had been born in Spa and educated in Warsaw. In 1907 he had become a Lutheran. He had gained the impression from his mother that his father's name was Borch, but as his mother was a Jew, the marriage wasn't regarded as legal. She later remarried. Baumberg had served for a year in the Russian Army and then travelled to Switzerland. He had arrived in England in 1910, and had been employed by Waring and Gillow (the furniture manufacturer) as a sales representative. He denied that he knew Baroness Baumberg was a spy, also known as Mrs Meyer, wife of New Yorker Henry James Meyer.

When police were called to Baumberg's room, they found him dead, and Malcolm having given himself up to PC Stevens. He said: "I want you to go to No. 3 Porchester-place. I have shot a man ... I suppose you had better have the revolver I shot him with." When police searched the dead man's room they found a substantial amount of correspondence from a number of women.

Malcolm's trial began at the Old Bailey on 10th September 1917. It was described as "one of the most sensational love tragedies of modern times" in the newspapers. The officials at the

Central Criminal Court had been overwhelmed with applications for seats from hundreds of people, but no tickets were issued for proceedings. The only people who would be in court were representatives of the press. The judge was announced as Mr Justice McCardie.

Sir John Simon, for the defence, produced a pistol which had belonged to Baumberg. Malcolm said: "I am not guilty" when asked how he pleaded. Mr Muir opened the case for the prosecution and related the by then well-known facts, saying: "prisoner had provocation of the most moving kind which any man could have, but it is not the sort of provocation which the law recognizes as being capable of reducing murder to manslaughter". Dr Spilsbury told the court that the first wound inflicted on the dead man had been fatal. Known as Bunny, Mrs Violet Brett was the first witness. She confirmed that she had met Mrs Malcolm one day as she was walking down Piccadilly. The two women, having been introduced, had become close friends, but Mrs Brett had asked Mrs Malcolm and the victim not to visit her at her home. On one occasion, however, they had arrived anyway. She told the defence that she had not known the two were lovers, and that when she had found out she had been shocked. When she had found them together they had both admitted their love for each other. The count had told Violet that he intended to marry Dorothy as soon as he could, but had added: "These people forced their ways on to me." She then sobbed passionately, but after composing herself, Violet recounted how she had been shown a loaded pistol by Baumberg. He had told his lover's friend that he had acquired the pistol in case he was attacked by Malcolm. She also told the jury that she had been present when Mrs Malcolm and the count argued over a German woman with whom he had had an affair. She agreed that Malcolm had done all he could to save his wife's honour, and his own. Baumberg, the court heard, was definitely of "worst character". Another witness told the jury that the German woman who had had a liaison with the count had been shot by the French.

Lieutenant Douglas Malcolm was found not guilty of the charge of murder on 11th September 1917. As soon as the foreman of the jury announced the verdict women and men jumped to their feet, clapped, stamped and shouted: "Hooray" as they waved hats and handkerchiefs. A man seated at the extreme end of the judge's bench cheered and waved a straw hat frantically. Pandemonium reigned for five minutes, while solemn ushers raised their arms and appealed in vain for order. The *Mirror* described the noise as "deafening" and the scene as resembling "the unrestrained jubilation of a pre-war football crowd". When the din had lulled a little, the judge spoke gravely, saying that he was sorry the annals of the court had been stained by such an outburst of applause. He said that the courts of justice should be conducted in a quiet, orderly manner.

Malcolm, however, stood impassive throughout. When the foreman announced the verdict a fleeting smile passed over his face and he glanced at the warder who stood by his side. He then resumed his grave demeanour, only occasionally raising his eyes to look at the cheering people around him. When the judge said: "Let Lieutenant Malcolm be discharged," he walked to the stairs at the back of the dock. He gave another faint smile, but otherwise his face was a mask of indifference. He was released by the public gallery entrance, and took a lone taxi ride after the dramatic end to his court case.

Because he was responsible to his superior military officers, Malcolm was unable to make any comments to the press on his release. The *Mirror* was informed, however, that the lieutenant was "extremely gratified by the way in which Sir John Simon 'absolutely cleared his wife's good name'".

# Michael Galvin and Thomas John Morris

1917

On 6th September 1917, a woman told an inquest in Birmingham that her struggle with two "housebreakers" resulted in the death of a seven-week-old baby. Following the child's death, two men were remanded in custody. Michael Galvin and Thomas John Morris were both present at the inquests as Minnie Lee, the mother of the baby, recounted what had happened.

The bereft woman told the inquest that when she had arrived home earlier in the week she had found the front door open and heard voices coming from upstairs. She had called out. One of the men said: "It is Alice," which was followed by loud laughter. Mrs Lee began climbing the stairs with her baby in her arms, and met the two men. As she hurried back down the stairs and into the kitchen, Morris caught up with her and struck her on the back of the neck, knocking her down. The baby's head bumped against the kitchen door in the fall.

Mrs Lee then attacked Morris. The two fought fiercely before Minnie saw Galvin take a hammer from his pocket. He swung it around to strike, but she couldn't say whether it struck her or the baby. She put the baby, now badly injured, on the floor and followed Morris into the yard before grappling with him again. They fought each other into the street; Minnie didn't know where Galvin was at this point. Morris then hit her in the chest and she fell to the ground for a second time. Her assailant then escaped.

Looking around the court, Minnie fixed her eyes on the two accused men in custody. "You are the man who has killed my child," she shouted, pointing to Morris. "I could fight him now," she said to the coroner. "You cannot realize what I went through." Mr Baker, who appeared for Galvin, said his contention would be that the accused was nowhere near the place. Mrs Lee, however, told the inquest: "I can swear to him. He brought the hammer. It is all clear before my eyes."

Dr Leather said that the baby's death was due to a fractured skull, one of the bones being completely broken in two. The injury was more likely to have been caused by a blow than by the fall

Home Front Killers

in the kitchen doorway. In reply to Morris, he said the fracture could have been caused by the mother dropping the baby if its head had struck against something. Morris made a statement admitting that he had entered the house, but said he had not seen a baby there. A verdict of wilful murder was returned against both men.

# The Great Sack Mystery
## 1917

On 2nd November 1917, detectives from Scotland Yard were busy trying to find clues to a "mysterious murder". The "Great Sack Mystery", as it was dubbed, was described by the *Mirror* as a "kind of super crime" containing "all the elements of a great drama". The newspaper wrote: "It reminds one of the sensational stories of Fergus Hume; it rivals Edgar Allan Poe in its weird details."

Early in the morning, in a quiet and little-frequented London square, a workman noticed a tied-up sack standing midway between a couple of trees. The peculiar shape and size of the sack caused the workman to stop, and an intuitive feeling told him that something was wrong. Fearing the worst, he ran until he found the nearest policeman, who returned with him and opened the sack, to find a "gruesome sight". It contained the nude and headless body of a young woman; her hands and feet were also missing, but they were found lying nearby a little later, tied in a brown paper parcel. The rain that had fallen during the night revealed footprints on the soft ground, and not far from the body a pair of boots were discovered. They fitted the dismembered feet of the woman in the sack.

The sack was discovered in Regent Square Gardens, situated in a "working class district" just off the Gray's Inn Road. It was renowned for being a quiet and lonely spot after nightfall. The sack, with its grim contents, had been placed about two yards inside the gate of the garden which occupied the centre of the square. It was typical of London squares of the time, with its grass, trees and bushes. Each resident had a key to the garden gate, which was padlocked every evening. On the morning the woman's body was discovered, the gate was open and the padlock and chain were missing. It was 8.30am when the workman saw the sack, and witnesses passing the gardens about an hour earlier were convinced that it hadn't been there then. A doctor called to the scene to examine the body found that the dismembered trunk was still warm. There was no confirmation of the victim's identity at this point, and her dismembered head remained missing. Two facts, though, were clear. First, the person who had severed the victim's legs, which were removed at the knee, had anatomical knowledge, and the limbs were cut from the body skilfully. Second, the legs had been removed so that the remains could be carried to where they were found.

Who the woman was and who murdered her baffled detectives,

but there were several theories. These included the possibility that the woman was a "foreigner" or that she was the victim of "the unwritten law". But these were only theories, and police had little in the way of clues to take their investigation forward.

On 5th November, the *Mirror* stated that the "Regent-square murder is proving to be one of the most baffling London mysteries of recent years". The victim was said to be around 30 years of age, but still remained unidentified. Her head and hands were still missing and the murderer, reported the paper, "is still at large". Scotland Yard's "keenest" detectives were hunting for clues, and on 4th November more than 100 people, including many women, had turned "amateur detectives". The searches for the missing body parts had been exhaustive, and unless some trace of them was discovered, it was going to be impossible to establish the identity of the victim. Police confirmed that their task was far from promising. The hands had been severed at the wrists, and police speculated whether they would be found with the head, or separately. They told the public that if the hands were in a parcel, it would be quite small. Obviously, they were easier to dispose of than the torso and the legs. A systematic search was conducted over open and waste spaces in the metropolitan area, but it would have been far easier, perhaps, for the murderer to dispose of the hands in the Thames. Police remained hopeful, though, that the woman would eventually be reported missing.

The body had been wrapped in sheets, but the laundry marks – if that's what they were – yielded no clues either. Even the name on the sacking which formed the outer wrapping of the body didn't provide anything useful. The sack was stamped "Joseph Rank, Ltd Premier Flour Mills, Broad Brand, 112lb. gross. Victoria Dock, London, E. D.3118," and while this gave the miller's mark, it didn't give any indication of who had possessed the sack once it left the company. The theory that seemed to "find most favour", the *Mirror* gathered, was one that associated the murderer with the butchers' trade. It was pointed out that the three pieces of white fabric known as "longcloth" in which the body was wrapped were of the kind that was usually wrapped around large portions of meat by wholesale butchers. This theory was also backed up by the clean and skilful severing of the limbs and head, which pointed to a knowledge of anatomy.

On 6th November, the day on which the inquest began, the *Mirror* reported that a butcher had been detained over the murder, and that the victim's identity was said to be "nearly established". The newspaper wrote: "Important developments took place yesterday in connection with the discovery of the headless and dismembered body of a woman ... last Friday. A man has been detained on suspicion by the police, and although the identity of the victim has not yet been established the detectives believe it will be proved that she was Madame Girouard, the wife of a French soldier." It had been the laundry mark "11 H", stitched in red cotton on the twill sheet which was wrapped round the remains, that had led to progress the previous weekend. The *Mirror* continued: "In the neighbourhood of Fitzroy-square linen similarly marked was discovered in a laundry. Mme Girouard had been missing since Wednesday, and the detectives sought to trace her all Saturday and Sunday, but without result. Her description so tallied with that of the victim that yesterday the police felt it to be only a matter of time before it is placed beyond doubt that it is Mme Girouard who has been murdered.

"Coincident with these inquiries was the detention at Bow-street of a butcher, believed to be a Frenchman. So far no charge has been preferred against him, but he has not been liberated."

The butcher was said to be a relative of the missing Frenchwoman, although police were prepared to find that this information was not correct. The *Mirror* gave an account of how the man was detained: "Chief Inspector Wensley and Divisional Detective Inspector Ashley went to his house in Charlotte-street. The man himself answered the knock at the door. 'We are police officers,' the detectives said, 'and are making inquiries in reference to the murder of a woman, part of whose remains were found in Regent-square on Friday morning. We propose to detain you on suspicion of having been concerned in it.' The man answered readily: 'I known nothing about it. I am innocent.' He was told that he would have to accompany the officers to Bow-street pending inquiries."

Meanwhile, a woman who lived next door to Mme Girouard in Munster Square said that the victim had occupied a room there for 10 months and that her two children had died. Adelaide Chester, who lived in the same house, said: "I have known Mme

Girouard for some time. She was rather a quiet woman and kept very much to herself. She could speak English slightly. I last saw her a week before she disappeared. I met her in a grocer's shop and asked her how she was. 'I'm all right,' she replied, 'but I feel so unhappy.'" Detectives took photos of the missing woman's apartments before padlocking the door. Mr Morgan, a dairyman who supplied Mme Girouard with milk, said that she was a very pretty woman. Her hands, he added, were heavily scarred, apparently from burns, and the marks amounted to a disfigurement, according to the press.

"Dramatic Sequel to Sack Mystery" wrote the *Mirror* on 7th November 1917, when it announced that the missing head and hands had been found. Slowly but surely, the story was beginning to unfold. When the inquest opened, the body was identified as that of Emilienne Gerard, a married woman, of about 30 years old. The coroner informed the jury that the missing body parts had been recovered and that two people had been detained by police in connection with the woman's death. One of the two detained was a woman. Both suspects were taken to Marlborough Street police court, and it was understood they would be brought before a magistrate on 7th November. The *Mirror* was informed that the head of the victim was found in a brine tub, and the hands in another. Noel John Joseph Brissi, who identified the body at the inquest, was from Belgium, and owned a Belgian café known as the Lenterne in Whitfield Street, between Tottenham Court Road and Charlotte Street. He said he knew the victim was married,

Home Front Killers

but only knew her husband's name as Gerard. He had last seen the victim alive on 31$^{st}$ October in a barber's shop on Tottenham Street – she was with a female friend who was due to travel to France. Asked by the coroner if Emilienne visited the café alone, Brissi said that sometimes she visited alone, and sometimes she arrived with or met a female friend there.

The workman, Thomas George Henry, who found the sack containing the mutilated body said: "There was nothing to suggest the contents of the sack, and I thought it was half a sheep or some beef. A man and woman were passing at the time, and I drew their attention to the package. The man smiled and went on; the woman stopped. I jumped over the railing, took my knife from my pocket, and cut the string of the wrapping, and found portions of a body wrapped up in what appeared to be a sheet." Although this was a little different from the first reported story of the finding of the torso, Henry confirmed at the inquest that he had found the woman's legs in a separate parcel a little way from the larger sack. He had noticed a piece of brown paper when he undid the sheeting that covered the woman's trunk, and was about to tell the coroner what the writing on the wrapping was when he was told not to say any more at that stage. Dr Bernard Spilsbury, who would later receive a knighthood, was already a well-known pathologist when he gave his evidence regarding the examination of the remains. He confirmed that the severing of the hands, legs and head had all taken place after death. The head and hands were found to be covered in a white powder mixed with sawdust, and after removal from the barrel in which they were discovered, he could see they had been lying on a thick bed of sawdust. The face and head were a mass of injuries. There were severe lacerated wounds and abrasions on the face as well as fractures to the right cheekbone. On the scalp there was a large lacerated wound at the back of the head and another lacerated wound on top of the head; these injuries were caused before death. The only signs of any kind of struggle were abrasions on the right hand, which suggested that the victim had tried to protect herself from the blows to the head. Dr Spilsbury confirmed that these had been numerous. The victim's French husband, who had been serving in France, arrived in the UK to give evidence at the police court proceedings.

More drama unfolded at Marlborough Street police court on 7th November when the arrested couple were brought before magistrates. Louis Marie Joseph Voisin (50), a stableman from 101 Charlotte Street, and Berthe Roche (38), a housekeeper at the same address, had to have proceedings translated from English into their native French. They were both charged with the murder of Emilienne Gerard. Voisin, described as heavily built, of medium height, with swarthy complexion and dark heavy moustache, wore a drab butcher's overall for his court appearance, while the accused woman wore a grey mackintosh and black hat and fur. The hearing didn't last long, but Chief Inspector Wensley told the jury that he and Detective Inspector Ashley and Superintendent McCarthy had picked up the cohabiting couple at their basement flat. Roche had been taken to Bow Street police station the day after her lover, and statements had been made through an interpreter. At the couple's address, police found the brine tubs – one of which was larger than the other – in a cellar connected to the basement. Inspector Wensley continued: "They have since been found to belong to the mutilated body which was found in Regent Square … Yesterday I conveyed the prisoners from Bow-street to Tottenham Court-road police station and charged them with the wilful murder of Mme Gerard. That charge was interpreted to them by Sergeant Quantrill. They made a reply in French to him. Later Voisin made a voluntary statement, which was interpreted and written down by Detective Sergeant Reid and signed." This was all the evidence that the police proposed to offer at this stage, so the magistrate asked if the accused wished to ask any questions. Neither did, so remand was set for seven days.

On 12th November, Paul Emanuel Julian Gerard, a French infantryman, attended the adjourned inquest and said: "I have seen the body in the mortuary, and I identify it as my wife." The accused couple were not present in court. Gerard spoke English well, and told the inquest that his wife was Emilienne Dumont (31). She had written to her husband to let him know that she had found employment as a servant in a house; she was employed at 101 Charlotte Street by Voisin. The accused man was described as having become friends with both Gerard and his wife. Mme Gerard had written several times to her husband after his return to the army that Voisin had been good to her, and had promised that he would find her husband a situation when he returned from the war. Three days later, Angelier Luppens, a porter at the address in Charlotte Street, was called to give evidence. The woman said that she knew Voisin's lover as Mrs Martin, and that she had been living in the house for the six weeks before the death of Emilienne. Luppens had been out all night before Emilienne disappeared, and when she returned in the early morning she had seen a light in Voisin's room. She had heard a great deal of noise coming from the basement, as if someone was "moving pots". She had met Mrs Martin in the house at around 8.30am, although Martin didn't normally surface until 9.30am or 10.00am. The witness asked the woman why she was up so early and was told: "Yes, Voisin came in just a minute before and he has just killed a calf and he is full of blood, and I washed his underclothes." Martin then went back to the basement with some water; she was seen at 10.00am washing Voisin's socks. Detective Sergeant Stephens told the inquest that there had been a smear of blood found in the dead woman's bedroom. The inquest also heard that when Emilienne was found there were some words in distinctive handwriting on a piece of brown paper with the body. Voisin was asked to write these words down at the police station, and Chief Inspector Wensley told the coroner that not only was the writing the same but also that the same words were incorrectly spelt in both cases. "I am of the opinion," the witness added, "that the writings are by the same person." The detectives told the coroner that when questioned, Voisin claimed that Emilienne had gone to Southampton, but they told him that she had been spotted at a house in London six hours after he said she had left. He didn't reply. In the stable, the police had found some butcher's tools, a knife, steel and saw, all wrapped in sacking. When questioned, Voisin said: "These articles came to-day from Surbiton. They belong to my employer, who has a farm there. I have been with him to-day killing a bullock." The police also told the inquest of their interview with Roche, who said she didn't know the victim. On being shown a photo of the dead woman, she said that she had never seen her or heard of her. Voisin had admitted knowing Mme Gerard for about 18 months.

On 21st November, the accused couple were charged on remand with the wilful murder of Emilienne. The jury did not believe that Voisin had killed a calf but that Berthe had been washing his clothes following Emilienne's murder. "My submission," said Counsel, "is that the blood on this shirt could only have come from the body of Mme. Gerard." Mme Gerard's heart also showed blood spots, which indicated that she had been partially strangled. Although there were no signs around her neck, Dr Spilsbury said it was quite possible that her head had been wrapped in the bloodstained towel to stop her from screaming. The victim's jewellery was found in a secret drawer under the mantelpiece of the accused's basement flat. In court, the jury also heard that Voisin was suspected of taking a letter from M. Gerard to his wife, which read: "My dear little Emilienne,

You did not tell me that Voisin had made you a present for your birthday. I doubt him a little, after all. You see, everyone thought of your birthday except me, but my heart thought none the less. I will make up for it ..." By this time, the police court also knew that one of the victim's earrings had been retrieved by police from the bloodstained towel. The other earring was still in the murdered woman's ear, attached to her severed head.

Voisin caused a sensation on 2nd January 1918 when he told the Marlborough Street police court: "I make the formal declaration that Mme Roche is entirely innocent." On hearing his statement, the accused woman burst into tears, leaning her head on the dock and sobbing bitterly for some time. Voisin continued: "The things that were found in Charlotte-street were taken from Mme Gerard's to my house. The murder was not committed at Charlotte-street but at Regent-square." Both prisoners were committed for trial.

In mid-January, when the case continued, the court was crowded at the Old Bailey for the first day of the trial. Both the accused pleaded not guilty. Mr R.D. Muir, for the prosecution, suggested that jealousy and a quarrel between Roche and Emilienne were the motive for the crime. The prosecution, he said, believed that the woman bled slowly to death and that the head was severed after death. He stated that Voisin had rehearsed the story which he told to his landlady that Emilienne had gone away on a holiday, and that 45 minutes before her remains were found he was seen by a police officer driving away from Regent Square.

After the three-day trial, Voisin was found guilty of the murder of the Frenchwoman, the jury taking just 15 minutes to reach their verdict. He was sentenced to death. Asked if he had anything to say, Voisin replied: "I have to say that I am innocent." Mr Justice Darling asked him if he understood English when spoken, and the convicted man replied in the negative. His Lordship accordingly passed the death sentence in French. Voisin turned pale on hearing his fate and gripped the front of the dock tightly. Berthe Roche was acquitted of the charge of murder, but was to be tried during the court's next sessions on an indictment that alleged she was an accessory. Voisin's death penalty, to be carried out on 26th February 1918, was adjourned until the following week on orders from the Home Secretary. He was kept at Pentonville Prison. On the day that he was to have been executed, Berthe Roche was amongst the prisoners at the Central Criminal Court Sessions charged with being an accessory after the fact. It was reported in the *Mirror* that Voisin was given respite so that he could give evidence at her trial. Roche stood in the Old Bailey witness box, and told the court how she had met Voisin four years before the murder. She said that on the night of 31st October she had got up at the sound of an air raid alarm and waited in the basement passage until the all clear was given, before returning to bed. Voisin was up early the next day – at his usual time – and went out. He returned at around midday, and said that he had been to Epping Forest to kill a calf. She had asked him why his knees were wet, and he replied that he had been to a friend's house to have a wash. She said he had left the house wearing one shirt and returned wearing another, telling her: "It was covered with blood, and so I had to change it." During the closing stages of her trial on 2nd March 1918, Roche listened as the defence, who eventually decided not to call Voisin (due to be executed the same day), argued that the Crown had absolutely failed to establish the guilt of his client. Mr Huntley Jenkins, defending, said that the fact Roche had been found with a trinket which had once belonged to the murder victim did not provide evidence that she had taken part in the murder. On the question of harbouring Voisin, he said that the jury must bear in mind the relationship which existed between the two. It amounted to that of "man and wife", and "that there had been nothing improper in his client's murder". He argued that the prosecution had built their case on theory. Voisin, meanwhile, met the gallows at Pentonville Prison.

# Mystery in Wimbledon

## 1917

Captain Edward Tighe was found in November 1917 lying on the floor of his bedroom at Winkfield Lodge, Wimbledon Common with serious injuries to his head. He died in hospital without ever recovering consciousness. Police stated they had no clues with regard to his murder, and confirmed it was "by no means certain" that the dead man's injuries had been caused by a bent poker found in the room. However, they did concede that the injuries were sustained by a heavy blunt instrument. As Captain Tighe's valuables remained untouched, robbery as a motive was instantly ruled out.

The inquest was set for 25th November 1917. The victim, cousin to the Earl of Bessborough, died four days after he was struck, but police had no motive for the murder. Whether a burglary had occurred or whether the case was something more sinister was still a mystery. The only items missing appeared to be a mackintosh, a small oxidized watch and a bunch of keys. Scotland Yard admitted it was baffled, although police were hopeful that one of their lines of inquiry would lead them to the killer. By this time, it was established that the captain had received eight severe blows to his head with the poker found near to his body. On 24th November, the *Mirror* wrote: "It is thought probable that the assailant, upon entering the bedroom while committing a burglary, was recognized by the officer, and in order to avoid detection, the intruder made sure that his victim would never live to give evidence against him." However, nothing new had been discovered when the inquest opened. The case was then adjourned for three weeks after Dr Collier had stated that the post-mortem examination revealed eight wounds on top of the skull. The first was a deep wound of 2½in that extended down to the bone. The other seven varied in length from 1½ to 2½in. The doctor said it was likely that the captain had been struck from behind and from the left side of his body.

On 13<sup>th</sup> December the *Mirror* reported: "The mysterious murder ... is apparently nearer solution. The *Daily Mirror* understands that a highly important clue has just been secured by Chief Inspector Gough and the other Scotland Yard detectives who have been grappling with the mystery for the past four weeks. Following on the pursuit of a certain line of inquiry by a large force of detectives, a foreigner was detained at Streatham in connection with a burglary. When the suspect's house was searched, police found the missing watch and mackintosh, believed to belong to the victim ... The *Daily Mirror* is informed that a sensational development may be expected at the resumed inquest."

The inquest opened again on the very same day, and a corporal in the British Army was brought before the police court charged with the murder of Captain Tighe. Arthur de Stamir (26), a French national, had been in the UK for many years. Chief Inspector Gough said that he had interviewed the accused at Streatham police station and told de Stamir that he was investigating the death of the captain. He explained to the court that police had found the accused with an envelope in the name of Ray, which gave a certain London address. After visiting the property, the police moved on to another house in the same street occupied by Neal McKinnon. In the pocket of a pair of trousers at the second property they had found a watch with the name "Angelus" on the dial and a serial number. "I produced another watch," said Gough. "This watch was found in a tin box with the clothes.

Among the articles found in that room which you occupied were a khaki coat and mackintosh, which I had laid on the table with other clothes in the room in [the] prisoner's presence." He then confirmed to the court that the coat and watch had been taken from Winkfield Lodge. The prisoner was then taken to Wimbledon police station and formally charged with murder. He said nothing, but was said to have made a statement on his way to the station, which he signed. The Frenchman was then held on remand. Towards the end of December the inquest heard what the statement contained when Sergeant Snaill read it out in court: "I entered the bedroom of Captain Tighe in company with another person. As the door opened the hall clock struck the half-hour and woke up Captain Tighe, who moved his hand along the pillow. It was understood that he had a revolver there. My partner did not wait, but struck Captain Tighe several blows on the head with a poker. Captain Tighe fell forward and struck his head against the fireplace. The room was then searched and we left Winkfield Lodge."

In the witness box, de Stamir said: "I agree that the statement by the police sergeant is correct." The coroner's jury returned a verdict of wilful murder against the accused and he was committed for trial.

In early January 1918, the accused man replied when asked about the charge of murder: "My defence is that the murder was committed by the other man." Mr Percival Clarke for the prosecution read the statement signed by de Stamir, who was then told that his trial would commence at the Central Criminal Court. On 12th February 1918, de Stamir was hanged at Wandsworth prison for the murder the previous November.

The court heard how the murder was "the climax to a life of crime". It transpired that de Stamir had been in trouble with the police in some form or other since his childhood. He was born in London to French parents and had given them trouble from the start. Before he was 14 he had been bound over on a charge of stealing, but within a year he had been charged and sent to a reformatory school for three years for burglary. On his release his parents had done their best to give him a new start. The *Mirror* wrote: "Their hopes, sympathy and encouragement were ruthlessly swept aside, and de Stamir, whose real name was Stamirowski, disappeared from home." Some months later his family discovered that he was in prison in Australia. "Then he disappeared," wrote the newspaper, "and was not heard of again until one morning he arrived in London." Despite his family's efforts to encourage the lad to start afresh, he refused to listen to their pleading. When war broke out in 1914 he enlisted in the County of London Yeomanry, but found himself in prison for "military offences" not long afterwards. He deserted within a few weeks of his release, was recaptured and then deserted for a second time. The *Mirror* stated: "Three-quarters of the time he was with his unit," but it seems that the rest of the time he was in prison for other military offences. Eventually de Stamir escaped from detention and went on the run. He occupied lodgings in various parts of London and stole to survive – he continued to wear his khaki uniform and posed as a corporal. While living with the wife of a soldier who was at the Front, he courted a young girl in a shop nearby, as well as other girls in Wimbledon and the surrounding district. He proposed to one young woman, who had started making wedding plans by the time of his arrest.

Meanwhile, in other news, Thomas Taylor from Leicester, who had been sentenced to death for the murder of his wife, was given a reprieve. His tariff was commuted to penal servitude for life. In Eltham, the inquest into the murder of Miss Nellie Grace Trew was opened, as Chief Inspector Carlin from Scotland Yard's CID continued with his investigation into the teenager's death.

# The Murder of Frances Elizabeth Earl

1918

A Canadian soldier was detained by the police in connection with the death of a young woman who was found with her throat cut, lying under a railway arch near Hackney Downs station, at the end of January 1918. When read the charge, the soldier told officers he was innocent, although in a statement he admitted to being in the dead woman's company the night before her body was discovered. He claimed that she was definitely alive when they parted company. She was said to be the wife of another soldier who was away fighting at the Front. Frances Elizabeth Earl, also known as Phyllis, had been married to Douglas Earl for some time when war broke out, but when her husband joined the colours she went out to work as a barmaid. She was unemployed – and had been for several months – at the time of her death.

George Harman (37), from the Canadian Expeditionary Force, was remanded in North London on 29th January 1918, charged with the wilful murder of Frances. Detective Inspector Pride said marks on the ground indicated that there had been a struggle and that the body had been dragged to where it was found. He sent a sergeant, accompanied by a Canadian military policeman, to fetch the prisoner, who confirmed that a knife found at the scene was his. When charged, Harman said: "If she done the same to me as she did I would do it again in the same way if she were alive." He was found guilty of wilful murder at the end of his trial in March 1918 and sentenced to death. He was later reprieved.

Earl was known to have given Harman a sexually transmitted disease after the couple had become engaged. He did not know during the initial stages of their relationship that the woman he lived with was actually married to someone else. He was known to be cross that he caught the venereal disease, and even more angry that Earl refused to see a doctor – shame, it seemed, had prevented her from seeking treatment. The jury asked the judge to show the convicted man "mercy" when they found him guilty of murder, because he had been living with a woman who had not only deceived him, but was also unfaithful to him. The people of London Fields, Hackney, petitioned for Harman's reprieve, stating that he had committed murder under extreme provocation. The fact that he had saved a woman's life some time before the war and had given up a good job in Canada to join the Canadian forces also helped to win the hearts of local residents.

# The Murder of Nellie Grace Trew

## 1918

On 12th February 1918 the *Mirror* wrote: "The police have in their possession what may prove a valuable clue to the murderer of Nellie Grave Trew, aged sixteen, whose body was found at Eltham Common, near Shooter's Hill, on Sunday morning." The girl, who had been a clerk at Woolwich Arsenal for six months, had been assaulted and strangled. She had left home at 7.00pm the night before she was discovered to go to Plumstead Library to change a book. She was expected home at around 8.30pm. "She was fond of walking, and according to her relatives was not afraid of the dark," continued the newspaper. Clenched in her hand, police found a regimental button and a brass metal regimental badge. It was clear that Nellie Trew had been on her way home when she was savagely attacked – she was just a few hundred yards away – but she was in a "lonely" spot, according to reports.

At the opening of the inquest on 13th February 1918, "a pathetic scene was witnessed" when the murdered girl's mother, Lena Trew, was called to give evidence. The woman, from Juno Terrace, Well Hall, Eltham, sobbed uncontrollably as she made her way to the witness box and continually cried out: "Oh God, help me." While it was difficult for her to overcome her emotions, she managed to give evidence, although she frequently broke down in tears. Nellie was known as Peggy, her mother told the court, and worked with her father at the Arsenal. "On the day she was born," said Mrs Trew, "my husband was reading a book called 'Peg the Rake.'" He had gone in to see his wife and baby daughter after the birth and said: "That shall be the baby's name." Mrs Trew continued: "When the war broke out, she felt that she must do something for the country and so she got work. Otherwise she would have been still at school. We were the best of chums." The coroner asked the victim's mother if Peggy had had any male friends or acquaintances, to which she replied: "No." She told the coroner: "She did not like men. She has often told me so. She just lived for her home ... she was everything to me." After Mrs Trew had given her evidence and the court had been informed about how the body was found, the inquest was adjourned for several weeks.

By 5th March, the day the inquest resumed, David Greenwood (21), a discharged soldier, was being held on remand on a charge of murder. He was present at the inquest. James Henry Green, a storekeeper at the Arsenal, said that a boy had told him about the discovery of the body; he had run up to the spot and picked up a button. "Was the button found after or before thirty or forty people crossed the field?" Greenwood inquired. "Afterwards," replied Mr Green. John Gibson, a manufacturer's manager, said that he had seen Greenwood wearing a "Tiger" badge – which was produced for the inquest – with a black bone button similar to the button found. The wire in the button was similar to that used in the workshop where Greenwood worked. The accused then asked to see the piece of wire and, borrowing a micrometer, he measured it carefully. A previous witness had already given evidence to say that the button wire was within one-thousandth of an inch of that used in the shop.

When the inquest was resumed again on 7th March 1918 by the Woolwich coroner, a lengthy statement made to the police by David Greenwood was read to the jury. On the way to Scotland Yard, Detective Inspector Brown, alongside Chief Inspector Carlin, noticed that the buttons were missing from the accused's overcoat. When queried about it, Greenwood said: "They have been off for a long time." The detective inspector also remarked that the overcoat was torn where one of the buttons should have been, and Greenwood replied: "That is where a button was pulled out, I suppose." He claimed that new buttons hadn't been sewn on to his coat because his mother was ill and "there had been no one to trouble about him." In his signed statement, Greenwood said that while going by tramcar to Woolwich on 9th February he was wearing his Leicester Regiment collar badge, and a man asked if he would sell it. He had bought the badge about six weeks earlier at a shop opposite Charing Cross underground station, but decided to sell it for 2s to the man, who claimed he had a son in the Leicesters. The statement continued: "The man seemed to be about medium height and middle-aged. I think he had a black overcoat and a bowler hat. He seemed well muffled up and to have a slight Belfast accent. He seemed by his manner to be a chap who lived in the open a great deal." Greenwood said that he had seen the photograph of the badge in the *Mirror*, and, thinking it was like the one he had sold, he went to the police to make a statement, on the advice of a colleague at Hewson Manufacturing Company, Ted Farrell. Meanwhile, Lieutenant Colonel C. Palmer, commanding the 3rd Battalion of the Leicestershire Regiment, wrote to the *Mirror* to point out that the description given of the badge – which represented an animal akin to a dog, sitting with its forefeet stretched in front of it – was not that of the Leicesters' tiger, which stood up with one forepaw outstretched.

The trial of David Greenwood took place in April 1918, and was adjourned for the second time at the Old Bailey on the 25th. The accused denied all knowledge of the crime, and explained his movements on the night of the murder. Asked if he could say whether the soldier's badge found close to the body of the dead teenager was his, he confirmed that he couldn't. When the trial resumed on the 26th, the principal witnesses were Greenwood's mother, sister and brother. He had given evidence that he was at home with his parents on the night of the murder, and his family, appearing on behalf of the defence, confirmed his alibi. However, the jury at the Old Bailey found Greenwood guilty of Nellie Trew's murder and he was duly sentenced to death. He was later granted a reprieve, and released at the age of 36 in 1933.

# William Hugh Cousins

## 1939

After sentencing a killer to death, Mr Justice Croom-Johnson returned to court at Wiltshire Assizes, Devizes, on Saturday 7th October 1939 to hear "remarks" the condemned man wished to make. The judge heard William Hugh Cousins (44), night watchman of Alderbury, near Salisbury, say: "I am sure and confident I had a very fair trial. I regret having caused a certain amount of trouble and worry to both families concerned, especially my own. I hope they will soon forget and forgive me for it. Ede was one of the pleasantest women and happiest women a man could have wished to live with. For that reason I am still willing and prepared to die for her only."

Edith "Ede" Jessie Cable (45) lived with Cousins in Alderbury for 10 years after the convicted killer had separated from his wife, who, it was alleged at the trial, he had also murdered. Cousins, the prosecution stated, shot his wife, Mary Ann Cousins (52), at her cottage in Durrington because she refused to divorce him, and that he shot Miss Cable because of jealousy. She was murdered in Ringwood, Hampshire, while Cousins was on his way to his wife's house. The dead woman was sitting beside him in the car. Sweet peas covered Ede's head when she was found. The defence contended that Cousins was insane at the time, but the jury refused to find a verdict of "guilty by insane". Cousins remained silent throughout the whole trial, except when he addressed his 14-year-old daughter who was in the witness box. He told her: "Speak up, Kathleen. There is nothing to be frightened of, my dear."

# George Quinnell
## 1939

A man accused of murdering his wife was said to have stated: "I idolized her. We have always been happy together." He was alleged to have confessed and added: "She was such a good wife. Why don't you kill me?" George Quinnell (59), described as an assistant storekeeper from Canal Road, Mile End, East London appeared at Thames police court and was remanded in custody for eight days. Divisional Detective Inspector Symes said that he had found Mrs Quinnell dead at her home. He later interviewed Quinnell at Arbour Square police station.

The officer read from a written statement which Quinnell had made: "I want to say what made me do it. I have lived with my wife for 37 years and I have been ill for months and had no sleep. I went to a nerve hospital because I was hysterical, and I gradually got worse. This morning my wife told me to go to Victoria Park for a walk. I went there, and stayed one and a half hours. When I came home she was cooking rabbit for dinner. I kept on thinking of leaving her as I had been so ill with an abscess. I thought I was going to die. I saw a Boy Scout's knife on the dresser. I had a terrible feeling I wanted to kill her, because I didn't want to leave her. As she was getting the rabbit out of the oven I stuck the knife in her throat. She fell on the floor, and I believe I struck her again. I went to Bow Police Station and told them what I had done."

There were no further reports in the newspaper about George Quinnell.

# Joseph Williams
1939

Guarded by three warders in Dorset Assizes court dock in Dorchester on 11th October 1939, Joseph Williams (70) earned the nickname "The prisoner who yawned on his trial for murder". His habit, it seemed, was infectious. A court official who happened to look at the accused in the middle of a long yawn could not prevent himself from doing the same. Williams yawned as the judge nodded to him to sit down after he had pleaded not guilty to battering in the skull of his affluent 64-year-old friend

Walter Alfred Dinnivan from Branksome.

On 21$^{st}$ May 1939 Dinnivan had been found dying with 16 head wounds in the sitting room of his flat by his 19-year-old granddaughter when she returned with her brother from a Sunday night dance. Williams also yawned as the prosecuting counsel Mr J.D. Casswell, KC, described Dinnivan's injuries, and how his assailant had tried to strangle him after rifling his safe and robbing the old man of jewellery and money. Williams' counsel, Mr J.G. Trapnell, KC, cross-examined Dinnivan's granddaughter, Hilda Dinnivan, about allegations that her grandfather received women visitors when she left him alone in the flat on her evenings off. Miss Dinnivan denied that he frequently received women. Mr Trapnell asked about a quarrel which Dinnivan had had with a lady called Mrs Watkins a week before his death. Mrs Watkins, it was stated, gave him electrical treatment and massage, and Dinnivan was said to be jealous of her relationship with another man. Hilda agreed that the row had been about the other man.

Statements by Williams were read to the court. The hearing heard that he declared it was preposterous to suggest that he had committed such a brutal crime. On that particular night he had gone for a walk to Bournemouth. "All along I knew I should be found not guilty, simply because I am not guilty. It was ridiculous to think I should murder anyone, let alone Mr Dinnivan, whom I had known for some many years," stated Williams. The retired fishmonger from Poole, Dorset, was speaking after his acquittal in mid-October 1939. Mr Justice Croom-Johnson, summing up, emphasized that the "long arm" of coincidence "would not do in this extraordinary case", and that there was no direct evidence. It took the jury 70 minutes to decide their verdict of not guilty. Susan Wilson, who had been Williams' housekeeper and who had given evidence for the prosecution, was one of the first to shake the freed man's hand. "Thank you very much, but I told you all along that I should be back," he told her.

# Dymitr Schreiber

## 1939

A seaman, enraged because his lover had been locked in her cabin for insolence to the captain, demanded her release and threatened to shoot the man in charge. When he tried to draw his revolver the captain shot him dead. The captain, Dymitr Schreiber, appeared at Southend on 27th October 1939 accused of murder. The magistrates decided that there was no case to go before a jury and he was discharged. Mr H. Robey, who prosecuted, said that the shooting occurred on the Polish steamer *Wigry*, which was in the Thames Estuary. The dead man was named as Jozef Jarosinski (34), a fireman on the ship; a stewardess was named in court as his lover. Jarosinski was said to have been drinking, and to have gone around the ship all day demanding her release. He was seen trying to hand the stewardess a revolver through a porthole, then moved towards the chartroom, and the first and second officers, who were both armed, ordered him back. He refused and they fired some shots wide. Captain Schreiber came on deck and ordered the bosun to search Jarosinski, who immediately put his hand inside his shirt as if gripping the butt end of a revolver. The captain immediately ordered the bosun to stand clear before shooting the seaman in the head and stomach. In a statement to police, Schreiber said: "Jarosinski came to the bridge and gave me 15 minutes to release the stewardess. He said he had a revolver. I asked him to show it to me and he pulled one from under his blouse."

# Maurice Sowerby
1939

"Tragic as the circumstances are, it can only be said that he killed his father not out of hatred for him, but out of love for his mother," said Mr Justice Macnaghten in a murder trial at Durham Assizes on 27th October 1939. The judge then made an order for the detention during His Majesty's pleasure of Maurice Sowerby (17), of Brusselton, Shilton, found guilty of murdering his father with an axe while he was asleep in bed beside his wife. Mrs Suzanna Sowerby said her husband was jealous of the children, addicted to drink and often abused the family.

# Thomas Albert Cossey

1939

A murdered woman's son and her mother were among those who signed a petition for a murderer's reprieve. Signatures were taken at the café where the condemned man and his victim had met and fallen in love. Thomas Albert Cossey (43), a fisherman from Grimsby, was condemned to death at Lincoln Assizes for the murder of Mrs Maude Steward, from Burgess Street, Grimsby. A strong recommendation to mercy accompanied the jury's verdict of guilty. Cossey and Maude had lived together for 12 months, but when the murdered woman fell in love with someone else, her lover killed her in a fit of jealousy in 1939.

"Cossey and Steward first met in my café," said Mrs Blood, owner of Betty's Café in Victoria Street, to the *Mirror* reporter on 3rd November 1939. "It was shortly after war was declared that he learned she had fallen in love with another man. That seemed to break him up completely. Mrs Batley, mother of Mrs Steward who lives in Hull, has told me that her name must on no account be omitted from the petition. Like all of us, she feels deeply sorry for Cossey, whose act seems to have been due to the fact that he loved too well."

Arthur Steward, the 19-year-old son of the victim, also chose to support the petition.

# Terence O'Brien

1939

In November 1939 a black cat strolled into the condemned cell at Strangeways jail in Manchester, where Terence O'Brien (28), an ex-soldier from Mill Street, Mossley, Lancashire, was awaiting execution for the murder of his wife.

O'Brien wrote from his condemned cell to his mother, Mrs Walker, from the same town, expressing hope that the black cat would bring him luck – and it did, in the form of a reprieve. Mrs Walker was overjoyed when told on 17th November that her son's life had been spared. "I had never given up hope that he would be reprieved," she said. "He shared this hope and has been cheerful throughout." She added that each time she had visited her son, and also in his letters, he had expressed a wish to see his 12-month-old son, and he was to be given an opportunity the following day when the baby was taken to the jail. O'Brien had been found guilty and sentenced to death at Lancaster Assizes on 14th October for the murder of his 20-year-old wife, Hilda, whom he strangled. The jury strongly recommended mercy – although an appeal against the sentence was dismissed. However, the sentence was commuted to penal servitude for life. It followed the news that Thomas Cossey had also been reprieved – the petition set up in the Grimsby café amassed 5,000 signatures and had been forwarded to the Home Secretary.

# Murder in Margate

1939

A man or woman murdered a victim, inexpertly sawed up the body, then threw the dismembered remains into the sea off the Kent coast. A reconstruction of the murder was outlined in the newspapers, which was thought to have taken place in the last few weeks of Margate's holiday period, immediately before the war and when the town was crowded with people. The first indication of the tragedy was the discovery of parts of a human body in a Corporation refuse destructor. Scotland Yard detectives, called in by the local force, then traced the corporation employee who had been clearing litter bins on the front at West Bay, Westgate – known as the fashionable end of Margate. On 10th November 1939 he told Chief Inspector Hatherill that he had seen what he thought was an animal carcass on the beach. He had tossed the remains into a litter basket on the promenade, half a trunk, thighs and knees. The following day, the remains passed through the screens and sifters of the destructor at Margate's refuse disposal plant. A workman who had first aid knowledge noticed the bones and the police doctors were called in. The incinerator was immediately stopped after the remains were found, and workmen sifted tons of refuse by hand in the hope of finding the remainder of the body, but without success. Chief Inspector Hatherill and Sergeant Orson, both from Scotland

Yard, and Chief Constable Palmer from Margate, stated that the parts of the body were from a "normal size adult", sex unknown. The rest of the body was still in the sea, they believed, and the action of the sea and sand during three or four weeks of stormy weather had made it difficult to determine anything more than that. "When I saw the remains I immediately recognized them as human and telephoned the police," said Mr A.H. Sayer, foreman of the destructor, who had 20 years' ambulance experience. Clumsy attempts had been made to dissect the bones. Every foot of the beach at Westgate was examined at low tides. "If a murder was committed and the body thrown into the sea," wrote the *Mirror*, "the killing and dismembering must have been carried out in the last few weeks of the pre-war holiday period."

Sir Bernard Spilsbury, the expert pathologist, made a detailed examination of the remains. He told police that the remains were those of a young woman, after examination of the body parts for more than two hours. Spilsbury took away pelvis bones for further tests, but did not reach a conclusion regarding how death occurred. Chief Inspector Hatherill and Chief Constable Palmer decided to await the preliminary post-mortem results before deciding whether the woman was the victim of murder, and talked over the case with Sir Bernard while they drove him back to London. Meanwhile, the search of the beach at Westgate was extended to Birchington and other areas of Margate, and it was reported that identification of the woman could not be made until more body parts were found. A check for missing people in the area was hampered because evacuation plans were already under way.

It was hoped that the post-mortem would reveal what had made the marks found on the dead woman's thigh bones. It was possible, police believed, that dismemberment could have been caused by the action of the sea and the surrounding rocks – in which case the woman could have been a passenger on a vessel who had fallen overboard. On the other hand, she could have been sawn or hacked up before being dumped in the waves.

What happened to the woman, and who she was, is not reported in any other editions of the *Mirror*, and reports elsewhere are severely lacking. This isn't surprising, given that Britain had just declared war on Germany. It was a difficult time for the press.

# The Murder of Charles Edgar (Chick) Lawrence

1939

Charles Edgar (Chick) Lawrence (36), from Hackney in London, was discovered battered to death in a courtyard off Lolesworth Street, Spitalfields, East London, in mid-November 1939. Police believed that he had been killed elsewhere and his body taken to the spot where it was found in a car. Chick was believed to have been involved with gangs in the area, and police reported that they thought he had been struck with a bottle in a local nightspot. He was an extremely powerfully built man, and was described as being a good match for at least two men. Several people must have seen his death, the *Mirror* stated, but it was thought that their fear of gang reprisals was keeping them silent.

Throughout the night during which the body was discovered, police called at lodging houses and questionable haunts, hoping to find someone who had seen the victim's body being removed from the spot where he had been murdered. They were still unable to trace the man's movements after he left a public house in Kingsland Road, Shoreditch, at 10pm on the Saturday night he died. It was thought that he went to at least one of the dubious "low-class" nightclubs in the area – which, although not licensed, sold drinks throughout the night to men who gathered there to gamble.

Members of London's criminal underworld were known to frequent these nightclubs, and police believed that Chick had been killed following an argument. They also thought that he may have "known too much" about particular criminals' acts. "Except for Saturday and Sunday he used to stay in each night," a relative told the *Mirror*. "On these nights he did not come in until the early hours. We have no idea where he went or who were his friends."

The methods Lawrence and his gang employed included protection rackets. Bookmakers were particularly affected by thugs who demanded money, and were often forced to buy "accessories at inflated prices". An attack made on a woman in Flower and Dean Street, close to the scene of the murder, was ruled out by police as having no connection with the crime. Superintendent Percy Worth, described as one of Scotland Yard's "Big Five", was in charge of the investigation.

# Private J. Humphries

1939

Firemen battering down the door of a blazing bedroom above a small shop in Stanningley, Leeds, found a 37-year-old woman stabbed to death and untouched by the flames. On 27th November 1939, just five hours after the discovery, her 18-year-old nephew, Private J. Humphries was arrested in York and brought to Leeds accused of the murder of his aunt, Miss Sarah Jean Brooks, of Coniston Mount, Stanningley. At Leeds police court, Detective Sergeant Craig stated that when arrested Humphries had said: "Yes, I did it." He was remanded in custody until December.

# Ernest Henry Lynch

1939

Letters left by a man found gassed with his wife in a sealed room showed that he had obtained the woman's discharge from a "mental institution" under a promise to "help her out".

The *Mirror* reported on Wednesday 6th December 1939: "On Saturday last I promised to bring her back to help her out and I have no compunction in doing so," the man wrote to his sister-in-law. "Try to forgive me if I have caused you any sorrow, but it will be better for Edie, and I have no intention of living without her; life would be too empty." Police found the couple, Ernest Henry Lynch (54), a painter, and his wife, Edith Georgina Lynch (55), dead in bed in a house in Foundry Lane, Southampton. On the floor, also dead, was the couple's pet cat. At the inquest on 6th December a verdict was returned that Lynch had murdered his wife and then committed suicide while of unsound mind. It was revealed that he was in despair over his wife's ill-health and his own unemployment. His wife had been a voluntary patient in a psychiatric hospital since attempting suicide in June 1939. The couple's letters were read at the inquest. Mrs Lynch had written to her sister: "Thursday – night of horrors. Awake all night. Day of horrors. Walking corridor. Counting spoons and forks. Washing up. No relief. Oh, God how much can I bear. Save me from life-long torture. No sweetness in life. Friday night – little hope. No relief. Torture and horror. Saturday no better. Oh, God, long for happiness. My poor health. No hope. Praying for relief. What can I do. God help me."

Lynch's letter to his sister-in-law began: "No doubt you will be horrified by what I have done before you read this, but believe me, there was no other way of solving our problems. In spite of the kindness of doctors and staff, Edie is not a bit better than she was when she made an attempt to end her agony in June."

# Petition to Aid
# Husband-Killer
1939

"Neighbours of a woman who was regularly thrashed by her husband over a 24-year period, and suffered in silence, were anxious to bring sunshine and happiness into the remaining years of her life," wrote the *Mirror* in early December 1939. Goaded beyond endurance, Annie Bell (50), of Drummond Street, Rotherham, Yorkshire, killed her husband with a hatchet. At Leeds Assizes on 6th December 1939 the murder charge was reduced to manslaughter and the convicted woman was sentenced to 12 months' imprisonment. Neighbours were said to be starting a "monster" petition for the woman who endured misery for so many years. Her daughter, 19-year-old Dorothy Steer, said: "I have sent a note to the judge thanking him for expressing sorrow for my mother. My little brother Desmond, aged five, keeps asking for his mummy. We have told him she is in hospital."

# Mother's Mercy
1939

A young widow was to offer a home to the man who unwittingly caused the death of her four-month-old baby in a "Friday the 13th" tragedy. Thomas Raymond Stell (22), an ex-sailor in the British Navy, appeared at Manchester Assizes on 7th December 1939 where he was acquitted of a charge of murdering the child. First to congratulate him was the baby's mother, Hilda Coggins, 33, from Berkeley Street, Salford. The woman, who had been widowed four years earlier, offered a home to Stell, the son of her best friend, when he was discharged from the navy in March 1939. Mrs Coggins told the court that her family of five young children worshipped Stell. When she went out to work after the birth of her baby in June 1939 he took care of the infant – but the child was found dead on Friday 13th October. The prosecution alleged that Stell had murdered the baby when he banged the child's head against the arm of a sofa. With tears streaming down his face, Stell told the court: "I had fed the child and was nursing him, but he kept on crying. I was kind of fed up, but I did not mean to harm him when I threw him on the sofa. I loved him too much." Mrs Coggins told the *Mirror*: "I am going to offer Tom lodging at my house again. He is a grand lad, and never meant to hurt my child." After being set free, Stell said: "I was twenty-two last Saturday and now I shall have to join up again. I shall go back in the Navy."

# Gordon Chilcott

1939

Opening the door of a saloon car parked in one of the lovers' lanes close to the sea front near Whitley Bay, Northumberland, a policeman found a girl dead in the back. Beside her was a young man, who was alleged to have told the officer: "I have choked her with my hands."

At Tynemouth police court on 15th December 1939, the man, who was named as Gordon Richard Chilcott (25), was remanded for seven days accused of the murder of Jean Watson Moore (21), daughter of an architect living in Lish Avenue, Whitley Bay. Jean was employed in Blyth, Northumberland as a shorthand typist. Tall, fair-haired and pretty, she was well known in Whitley Bay, and friends described her as "happy and jolly". A few weeks before her murder, Jean joined the WAAF and was stationed at Blyth. Chilcott was also fairly well known amongst his peers on the coast.

Constable Beal told magistrates that at 12.50am on 15th December 1939, on the road leading from Broadway to Marden Farm, Cullercoats, he had found the car "standing without lights". He found the young couple on the rear seat. The inquest into Jean's death opened on 16th December.

Chilcott, an estate agent, was charged with her murder, while the inquest heard that the young woman had been "interfered with". Prosecutor Mr E.G. Robey stated that the couple had become engaged two years earlier, but that some days before the tragedy the relationship had been "broken off". Chilcott was said to be depressed about it, regarding the matter as one that couldn't be "patched up". On 14th December, Jean and her colleague Patricia Svenson went to a dance at the Whitley Bay Hotel. Witnesses described the ex-lovers as apparently happy to be dancing together, until 11.00pm when the dance ended. Less than two hours after the dance ended, Jean was found dead. Chilcott, from Naters Street, Whitley Bay, was sent for trial at Northumberland Assizes. Chilcott had taken Jean and Patricia in his car to his ex-lover's home, where Patricia had got out of the car. At 12.50am the car was discovered by Constable Beal, about half a mile from Jean's home. Dr J.T. Philips said that the girl had died from asphyxiation and that there was evidence of sexual assault.

On 3rd February 1940, the court heard that Chilcott had been aware that Jean wanted to have "a small fling" before she married. After killing her, the estate agent decided to commit suicide, but he decided to have a last cigarette first. It was while he was smoking that Constable Beal opened the door of the vehicle. He was found guilty of murder at Newcastle Assizes and condemned to death. Chilcott had pleaded not guilty at his trial. He had told the jury that he had met his ex-lover four years earlier, and that they had spent all their evenings together until she joined the Wrens in 1939. He had heard gossip that while

George Joseph Smith murdered three women after taking their life savings and then claiming their life insurances.

"Brides in the Bath" murderer George Smith with victim Bessie Munday in 1910.

PIRATES SINK 3 MORE BRITISH STEAMERS

# The Daily Mirror

CERTIFIED CIRCULATION LARGER THAN ANY OTHER PICTURE PAPER IN THE WORLD

3,549.    WEDNESDAY, MARCH 10, 1915   **16 PAGES.**   One Halfpenny.

## REMARKABLE DEVELOPMENT IN DEAD BRIDES' CASE: STORY OF THREE OTHER MARRIAGES AND A WIFE IN CANADA.

*John Lloyd*

The front page of the *Mirror* breaks the astonishing news of more of George Smith's marriages.

Evidence produced during the trial of George Smith showing the marriage certificates of his weddings to May Tanner (top), where his name appears as Charles Reginald Russell, and Margaret Elizabeth Lofty (bottom), where his name appears as John Lloyd.

An array of Mrs Smiths ... or Mrs Lloyds – depending on which name he was using! Edith Pegler, Alice Burnham, Alice Reavill and Caroline Thornhill.

The accused man watches from the dock during his trial in 1915.

The front page of the *Mirror* dated Friday 2nd July 1915 announces that George Joseph Smith had been found guilty of murder and sentenced to death.

GERMANS SINK ANOTHER LINER WITH AMERICANS ON BOARD

# The Daily Mirror

CERTIFIED CIRCULATION LARGER THAN ANY OTHER PICTURE PAPER IN THE WORLD

THE MURDERER IN "THE BRIDES IN THE BATH" CASE SENTENCED TO DEATH AT THE OLD BAILEY.

*Joseph Smith*

*H. Williams*

Margaret Ellen Nally was found strangled in the ladies' waiting-room at Aldersgate Street station. The little child was only seven years old the day before she met her death. It was supposed that she was enticed away by a man masquerading as a woman.

Participants at the inquest into the death of Maggie Nally in June 1915.

THE STATION MURDER INQUEST: CHILD WITNESS WHO WOULDN'T SPEAK.

The child's mother and father

ID ACQUITTED OF MURDER CHARGE AT OLD BA

er.                Miss Wheatley and her counsel after the trial.              Lieu

llowing the acquittal of Alice Mary Wh
ed for the murder of Annie Wootten, th
Albert Wootten.

raph taken the day before murdering h
ing suicide, Ada Ann Elms poses with
lizabeth (9), Thomas (6), Alfred (3) a
).

A cap and coat found when sp... constables sear... the woods near... St Albans in Ma... 1917 for any cl... which might he... to solve the my... surrounding the murder of Janet Oven.

...n-year-old Albert Edward Lorford is remanded in ...y over the murder of Janet Oven. Lorford was ...ally found guilty of manslaughter and sentenced ...years.

# The Daily Mirror

CERTIFIED CIRCULATION LARGER THAN THAT OF ANY OTHER DAILY PICTURE PAPER

No. 4,313.  Registered at the G.P.O. as a Newspaper.  TUESDAY, AUGUST 21, 1917.  One Penny.

## THE MALCOLM CASE: JUSTIFIABLE HOMICIDE VERDICT

Mrs. Malcolm, who gave evidence at the inquest yesterday.

Lieutenant Malcolm, the accused. He made a brief appearance in the dock at Marylebone yesterday.

Anton Baumberg.

Detective carrying a hunting crop, one of the exhibits.

Miss Kate Knight.

A verdict of Justifiable Homicide, the act being committed in self-defence, was returned yesterday at the inquest on Anton Baumberg, a Russian, known as "Count" de Borch, who was found shot dead in his room at a Bayswater boarding - house. Lieutenant Douglas Malcolm, R.F.A., who stands remanded on a charge of murdering him, made a brief appearance at Marylebone Police Court. Miss Kate Knight, of the Censor's Department, who gave evidence during the week end, stated that she saw a man enter the house where she and the deceased were boarders, with a hunting crop under his arm. This was produced at the Coroner's Court yesterday.—(Daily Mirror photographs.)

The key players in the murder of Anton Baumberg in August 1917, as the paper announces the court's verdict of

HAIG'S NEW BLOW—BERLIN: 'TAGLIAMENTO OURS

# The Daily Mirror

CERTIFIED CIRCULATION LARGER THAN THAT OF ANY OTHER DAILY PICTURE PAPER

No. 4,380.    Registered at the G.P.O. as a Newspaper.    WEDNESDAY, NOVEMBER 7, 1917.    One Penny.

## PICTURES OF THE REGENT SQUARE MURDER MYSTERY

The house where the detained man lived. At the back are the stables.

Mme. Emilienne Gerard, whose body has been identified as that of the murdered woman.

The shelter where portions of the body were found.

Mr. Alfred Henry, the man who discovered the body of the woman in Regent-square, King's Cross.

Detective Inspector Wensley, who is in charge of the case. He has had a long and varied experience in criminal investigation.

The police have succeeded in discovering the head and hands of the woman whose body was found in the gardens of Regent-square last Friday morning, and are now practically satisfied that the victim was Mme. Emilienne Gerard, who had been missing from her house since the date of the murder. In addition to the man already detained in connection with the mystery—a butcher, named Louis Voisin—the police have detained a French widow, named Mme. Roche Martin. M. Paul Gerard, the husband of the missing woman, who is serving with the French Army, has been granted leave to come to London for the purpose of identifying the remains.—(Daily Mirror photographs, etc.)

London was gripped by the discovery of a woman's dismembered body in Regent Square in November 1917. The victim was later identified as Emilienne Gerard.

"SHE IS INNOCENT."

Frenchman Louis Marie Joseph Voisin was later hanged for Emilienne Gerard's murder, but a lack of evidence against his alleged accomplice Berthe Roche allowed her to walk free.

Canadian soldier George Harman (right) was charged and convicted of the murder of barmaid Francis Elizabeth Earl in January 1918.

Jean Watson Moore died in a Whitley Bay "lovers' lane" in December 1939. Gordon Chilcott admitted killing the 21-year-old and was planning on committing suicide, but was apprehended while enjoying a final cigarette.

Lady Cayzer – wife of Sir Char[les]
Cayzer (44), baronet and MP [for]
Chester – was widowed after h[er]
husband was found dead at th[e]
Kinpurnie Castle home in An[gus,]
February 1940.

DAILY MIRROR, Thursday, MARCH 14, 1940.

# Daily Mirror

MAR 14

No. 11,315 — ONE PENNY
Registered at the G.P.O. as a Newspaper.

# ASSASSIN
# SHOOTS MINISTER,
# KILLS KNIGHT

SIR MICHAEL O'DWYER, AGED SEVENTY-FIVE,
GOVERNOR OF THE PUNJAB DURING THE
AMRITSAR RIOTS IN 1919, WAS SHOT DEAD BY
AN INDIAN GUNMAN AT A CROWDED MEETING
IN CAXTON HALL, WESTMINSTER, YESTERDAY.

The gunman fired first at Lord Zetland, Secretary of
State for India, and slightly wounded him. Then, as they
rose to reach him he turned his gun, shot and wounded
Lord Lamington, aged seventy-nine, ex- Governor of Bombay, and Sir Louis Dane, aged eighty-four, another Punjab ex-Governor.

Nearly 300 men and women had heard Sir Percy Sykes
address the meeting of the East India Association in the
Tudor Room of Caxton Hall.

Lord Zetland was in the chair.
Lord Lamington had risen to propose a vote of thanks, when a
thick-set Indian rose, walked to the Press table, pulled out a revolver and fired.

As the first two shots were
fired Lord Zetland toppled over
and collapsed on the arms of his
chair.

Sir Michael O'Dwyer jumped
up. Two shots entered his
heart and he fell back dead.

## Assassin Fired
## Six Shots

The assassin fired six times.
With his last two bullets he
wounded Lord Lamington and Sir
Louis Dane, who had been sitting
at each end of the front row of
the audience.

Sir Louis was hit in the arm;
Lord Lamington's right hand was
shattered.

For a shocked second no one
moved. The assassin paused, studied
"Make sure, make sure," and dashed
down the aisle.

Two men, one of them in uniform,
jumped on a man and threw him.
Then men and women jumped to
their feet, shouted "Murder, police
. . . a doctor."

Sir Michael O'Dwyer—died with
two bullet wounds in his heart.

Thirty-seven-year-old Indian, Mahomed Singh Azad, leaving the Caxton
Hall with police. He was charged last night with the murder of Sir
Michael O'Dwyer and with wounding Lord Lamington, Sir Louis Dane
and Lord Zetland by meeting them with a revolver.

Lord Zetland—a
bullet graze' his
ribs, and he fell

(Continued on Back Page)

Lord Lamington
was shot in the
hand.

# FINN, SWEDE,
# NORWAY PACT

A CONFERENCE between Finland, Sweden
and Norway for the conclusion of a treaty
of defensive alliance will be opened immediately, declared M. Tanner, the Finnish Foreign
Minister, in Helsinki last night.

M. Tanner stated that the war with Russia had
presented the investigation of the possibilities of
such a pact, which he said "will secure the fron-
tiers and the independence of these three nations."

## Soviet-Rumanian Treaty

He added that it had been agreed by the Govern-
ments of the three countries that now a Russo-
Finnish peace has been re-established, the question
of an alliance should be investigated.

Plans for a non-aggression pact between Russia
and Rumania were reported in Bucharest, Rumanian
capital, last night to be under consideration. The
talks would be held in Berlin.

A military commission composed of high-ranking
Rumanian Army officials is at present in Berlin. The
Rumanian delegation is reported to have left for
Berlin secretly, says the Associated Press.

Sweden to Rumania From France—Page 2.

## Keep smiling

## Guinness is good for you

The front page of the *Mirror* breaks the news of the
assassination of Sir Michael O'Dwyer in March 1940.

Constance Ison's body was found in a locked wardrobe at a house in Brighton in March 1940. Hilda Mary Morgan, a housekeeper, was charged with her murder.

Julia Ransom was charged with the murder of three women found at a lonely farmhouse in Crittenden in Matfield, near Tonbridge in Kent, in August 1940. Ransom was later certified insane and sent to Broadmoor.

Fifteen-year-old Mary Hagan's body was found in Liverpool in November 1940. Despite protesting his innocence until the very end, Samuel Morgan (27), was convicted of her murder and later executed.

Former beauty queen Sybil Ann Chilvers (25) was found by police lying dead on her living room floor in March 1941. Her husband, Donald Chilvers, was found guilty of stabbing her to death, declared insane and detained at His Majesty's pleasure.

Dr Harold Trevor – a philanderer and fraudster – was charged with the murder of Theodora Greenhill in October 1941.

Gunner Harold Hill being led away in handcuffs from Chesham Police Court, Buckinghamshire, in December 1941 having been remanded and charged with the murder of Doreen Hearne (8) and Kathleen Trendell (6).

Following the guilty verdict against Harold Hill in March 1942, Mrs Hearne (centre) embraced the murderer's mother while Mrs Trendell waits to tell her "We have no malice towards you."

The Blackout Ripper was the nickname given to 28-year-old Gordon Frederick Cummins, an English serial killer who murdered four women in London in 1942.

Three of Cummins' victims – Evelyn Oatley, Doris Jounannet and Evelyn Margaret Hamilton. The Blackout Ripper was executed for his crimes in June 1942.

Caroline Trayler, a Folkestone usherette, was found dead in an empty bomb-damaged shop four days after she was reported missing in June 1943.

Iris Miriam Deeley was murdered by Gunner Ernest James Harman Kemp of the Royal Artillery on Valentine's Day, 1944.

Officers remove Deeley's body from where it was discovered near Well Hall railway station, Eltham.

Mourners at Iris Deeley's funeral at Manor Park Cemetery, 18th February 1944.

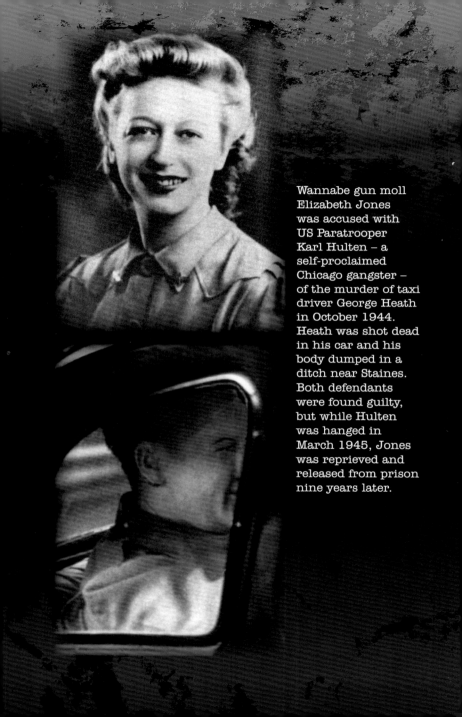

Wannabe gun moll Elizabeth Jones was accused with US Paratrooper Karl Hulten – a self-proclaimed Chicago gangster – of the murder of taxi driver George Heath in October 1944. Heath was shot dead in his car and his body dumped in a ditch near Staines. Both defendants were found guilty, but while Hulten was hanged in March 1945, Jones was reprieved and released from prison nine years later.

out with friends she attended dances and was often seen talking to other men, and this led to a quarrel between the couple. Three days before their final meeting, Jean had written: "Darling, I have more courage on paper than I have when I am with you. Just to be near you sends all my resolutions up in smoke. I feel that I want a few months freedom just to be like other girls and have a very small fling before I marry. After all, darling, you have had yours." Chilcott told the court he had nothing but affection for Miss Moore. Describing the events in the car, he said that Jean had started to struggle a little but soon became limp. "Afterwards," he declared, "it occurred to me that something had happened. She did not respond to my shaking her and I realized she was dead. I thought a while and decided to take my own life. I had a knife and got it out to use, but decided to have a cigarette first. The policeman came up before I had finished the cigarette." Chilcott said he had no idea what killed the girl, and that he did not knowingly suffocate Jean. Under cross-examination he said that he told the police officer that he had choked her because he thought that if he didn't have the courage for suicide he would plead guilty in court. He changed his mind because he was advised he might not be able to plead guilty, and he didn't want to be given penal servitude.

Chilcott was to be executed for Jean's murder in Durham jail on 28th March 1940 at 8.00am. His appeal a month later failed. He received a reprieve on Good Friday after 5,000 signatures, which included those from psychologists, doctors, solicitors and councillors, to save his life were received by the authorities within a two-day period.

# Missing Boy Found in Well

1939

A teenager of 15 was charged on 15th December 1939 with the murder of a seven-year-old child who was found dead at the bottom of a well near his home. The murdered boy was Dereke Saunders of Nine Ashes, Blackmore, Essex, who had been missing since 6th December. The youth was charged at a special court at Ongar, Essex and remanded until the following week. Detective Sergeant Jeavons said that the body was found at 3.15pm – the same day the 15-year-old was charged – inside the well at Paslow Hall Farm. Later, Jeavons and other officers interviewed the accused youth. – and the teenager had admitted that he struck the victim over the head with a bottle before pushing him into the well.

At the inquest, which opened on 18th December, it was revealed that the child had not died from drowning, but from a blow to the head. Dr F.E. Camps said that death was due to shock caused by being struck, which resulted in a fractured skull and lacerated brain. Detective Sergeant Jeavons told the inquest the child had been missing for nine days, and that search parties had been organized throughout that time. Dereke was eventually found floating in 23in of water in a 4½ft deep well just one mile from his home. The inquest was adjourned pending criminal proceedings.

Errand boy George Robert Saffill was ordered at Essex Assizes at Chelmsford to be detained at "a proper place" during His Majesty's pleasure on 6th February 1940. When Saffill pleaded guilty to the murder of Dereke, the judge, Mr Justice Charles, told him: "You will be looked after and I hope that any sickness of mind you have will be removed." Mr J.C. Llewellyn, on behalf of Saffill's parents, expressed their sympathy for the parents of Dereke Saunders.

# Sydney Charles Pitcher

## 1939

"I thought he was getting more attention than me, and it made me jealous of him. I used to think about it at work every day and it played on me." This alleged statement was read at the North London police court on 27th December 1939 when Sydney Pitcher (41), a painter living at Terrace Road, Hackney, East London was committed for trial, charged with the murder of Arthur Thomas Haberfield. Counsel stated that Haberfield occupied a newsagent's shop in Terrace Road, where Pitcher and his wife rented rooms. The two families had been friendly for years. Referring to the night of the murder, Pitcher's statement continued: "Arthur came in just after eight, and we sat round the fire. Arthur and my wife were talking. When he was talking he got hold of my wife by the arm. It worried me because I had previously told him he wanted to be too intimate with my wife, like he was with the women in the shop. My wife did her hair in the kitchen and went to bed leaving me in front of the fire and Arthur sitting in the armchair. Something came over me; God knows what it was. A sort of dark cloud came up and God above knows what happened to me."

At Pitcher's trial, which opened at the Old Bailey in January 1940, a further statement made to police was read out: "I didn't like the way he had of touching women on their arms and shoulders when they came into his shop. I thought he would be doing the same to my wife. It played on me, although I knew my wife would do no wrong." After Arthur's wife and children had been evacuated, he stayed with Sydney Pitcher and his wife, but jealousy was beginning to put a strain on the two men's relationship. The prosecutor said that it was this jealousy that drove Pitcher – a man of exemplary character and a good husband – to kill his friend with a knife. Mrs Pitcher told the court: "My husband was extremely jealous but I never gave him cause." She said that one day she had taken Arthur Haberfield a cup of tea, and when she returned her husband had become hysterical and cried. Suddenly he jumped up and clasped her round the throat.

She cried: "Oh Syd!" and punched him; he released her and asked her to forgive him. Once he had exclaimed that God must help him to overcome his jealousy. The police said that in his statement Pitcher showed his extreme emotions over the matter and stated that he didn't know what he was doing as he killed his friend. The jury at the Old Bailey found the accused guilty but insane. Mr Justice Tucker ordered him to be detained during His Majesty's pleasure.

# The Murder of Elsie Mary Ellington

1940

A boy of seven heard shouts and ran into the scullery of his home on 16th January 1940, to find a young woman who lodged with the family dead from what appeared to be knife wounds. Philip Brigdon, from Inville Street, Southwark, southeast London, ran upstairs to his mother who was ill in bed and shouted: "Miss Ellington is lying down and bleeding." The 27-year-old victim, the assistant manager of a Camberwell café, had been lodging with the Brigdon family for 18 months. Ernest Hamerton (35) was later arrested in connection with the murder and was taken to Carter Street police station in Southwark. He was to appear before Lambeth police court the following day. Elsie had been off work for five weeks on sick leave. Although she hadn't given any real details, her friends and the women where she worked had heard her talking about becoming engaged and married before the year was out. Mrs Brigdon had asked Elsie to prepare breakfast because she herself was unwell on the morning of the tragedy. When her son told her what had happened she immediately sent for the police. Superintendent Young, together with fingerprint experts and photographers from Scotland Yard, arrived at the scene, while later Manchester police interviewed a man they thought could assist in the inquiry. Elsie had previously lived with her parents in Blackpool, but when they moved to Barrowford near Nelson, Lancashire, she rented a room in her home town where she worked in a teashop. She was promoted to one of the firm's London shops.

A neighbour said: "She was a quiet, attractive girl and rarely went out in the evening. She used to say that she preferred to stay at home and read." During the investigation the police took away a number of letters found in Elsie's bedroom. Hamerton (25), a kitchen porter, was alleged by police to have said: "All right. I have given up all I had for that girl." When charged, he said: "That is quite correct." Divisional Detective Inspector White confirmed that the accused would remain on remand until Friday 26th January.

On 27th January 1940 the *Mirror* reported on a statement by Hamerton, which read: "She promised to marry me and then turned me down flat. I lost my head and just did it. It's no use – you can't pick up spilt milk. I will have to pay for what I have done." The police alleged the statement was made after the accused's arrest. Hamerton was sent for trial the day before the newspaper report. Meanwhile, it was revealed that Elsie had been found with a knife sticking in her left breast. The last words she uttered as she lay dying were for her lover: "You bad ..."

On 8th February, Hamerton was sentenced to death for the crime. He said: "If I had lived, those words would have haunted me to the grave." After sentence had been passed, Hamerton turned to the judge and said: "Thank you, sir." As he was taken down, the convicted man was smiling.

At the Old Bailey the day before, Hamerton had pleaded guilty to the murder, but on 8th February he changed his plea to not guilty. The young couple had met in Lancashire, and he had moved to London when Elsie was promoted. When Elsie ended the relationship it had led to a quarrel. He told the court: "I meant to kill her, and I did it. I ask for no leniency." Ernest Hamerton was executed on 27th March 1940.

# Child Murder Charge
1940

Patricia Mary Proctor (30), wife of a bank clerk from Withy Close East, Westbury-on-Trym, near Bristol, was remanded at Bristol police court on 5th February 1940 accused of strangling her only child, also Patricia Mary Proctor, aged five. Proctor leaned heavily on the arm of a policewoman as she came up the stairs from the cells and throughout the hearing, which lasted three or four minutes, she stood in the dock and stared straight ahead as if in a daze. Proctor's husband said that his wife was "over devoted" to the child when she was committed for trial on 13th February. Mr G.R. Paling, prosecuting, said her mental condition would have to be inquired into.

Mr Proctor had returned home after receiving a call from his wife, and as he went upstairs, she hit him several times on the head with a hammer, alleged the prosecutor. A doctor said that when Mrs Proctor saw him sometime before the child's death, she was "suffering from a mental disease". He warned the Bristol court that there was a grave risk of the accused committing suicide. There were no further news reports on the story.

# Jacintha Rogers
1940

"In the cold, brutal language of the law," said the coroner on 8th February 1940, "Mrs Rogers murdered her husband and then committed suicide." The Teignmouth inquest heard that Jacintha Rogers from Shaldon, Devon murdered her officer-husband as he lay asleep because she loved him too much. He was due to return to his official duties that day and she couldn't bear to be parted from him, the inquest was told. Captain Thomas Rogers and his wife, both aged 35, were deeply in love. Every day that he was away on active service the couple wrote to each other, and they also spoke every evening on the phone. Rogers was worried about her husband's health, and when he returned home on leave in late January she was overjoyed.

On the day that Captain Rogers should have returned to his unit, a close friend of the couple phoned their cottage and received no reply, so he called on Brookvale Cottage and found that their pigeons were hungry and the curtains of the cottage were drawn. He was suspicious and decided to enter the house. When he went into the bedroom and switched on the light, he discovered Rogers lying on the bed grasping a double-barrelled sporting gun. She was dead. In the adjoining bed was her husband, also dead. "From his position and his peaceful expression I believe that he was shot at point-blank range while asleep," stated PC Prior, who was called to the cottage following the tragic incident. "I believe he was shot by Mrs Rogers who discharged the weapon while kneeling on her own bed. From the position of the gun, I think she afterwards took her own life."

In the dining room PC Prior found a note in Rogers' handwriting that said: "Mary Rose is with her grannie, The Manor, Homington, Salisbury." Mary Rose was the couple's seven-year-old daughter, who had been sent to stay with her grandparents, Brigadier General and Mrs Gordon. The coroner handed the jury copies of a letter written by Rogers to her husband. "I'm not going to read it," he said, "because I think it is too sacred a document, but I want you to see it because it will give you some indication of the kind of lady she was." He continued: "the jury will be satisfied that the two were a devoted couple to whom separation was painful. The letter showed she was deeply religious and breathing utmost affection for her husband." The jury found that Captain Rogers was murdered by his wife, who then committed suicide while the "balance of her mind was disturbed by acute depression".

# Joseph Myatt

## 1940

A man of 36 who had "the mind of a child of twelve" killed a woman and thought his punishment would be a fine of 5s, Derby Assizes was told on 19th February 1940. Joseph Myatt, a farm labourer from Congleton, Cheshire, was sentenced to death for the murder of Fanny Stevens from Ockbrook, Derbyshire. The jury made a strong recommendation "to mercy" and Mr Justice Oliver said it would be forwarded to the "proper quarter". Mr O'Sullivan, prosecuting, described the woman as one of the "unfortunate class", known in the 21st century as a sex worker. Her body lay for six days under some hay in a field in Breadsall, Derbyshire. Police Sergeant Fairbrother said that Myatt at first denied having seen the victim, but later said his statement consisted of lies. Myatt added: "I simply lost my temper. I kicked her in the face as she lay down. I put paid to her by finishing her off with the heel of my shoe. Her scarf was around her neck and I tied it and covered her with hay." Mr N.T. Winning, defending, said that a doctor who had examined Myatt described him as having the mind of a child. Dr C.M. Dickinson from Leicester jail said that an aunt and uncle and two cousins of the convicted man had spent time in psychiatric facilities. Myatt was described as an "inveterate liar" and no reliance could be placed on virtually anything he said. The doctor added that the convicted man would have known what he was doing to the victim, and that he did know the difference "between right and wrong". Mr Winning said there was no evidence against Myatt except his own contradictory statement. The case was not the first time he had confessed to murder.

# Baronet and Butler Found Shot

1940

United in grief, the widows of a baronet and his butler who died together met at the baronet's castle on 19th February 1940 to exchange expressions of sympathy. Lady Cayzer, widow of Sir Charles Cayzer (44), baronet and MP for Chester, of Kinpurnie Castle, Angus, and Mrs Wexham, widow of Benjamin Wexham from London, met after their husbands were found shot in the butler's pantry. Mrs Wexham, accompanied by her nephew, arrived at the village station after a day's journey from London. They were met by Lady Cayzer's chauffeur and driven to the castle. At this point, Mrs Wexham was unaware that Sir Charles was dead. Both men had suffered severe gunshot wounds in the head. Shortly before the murders Sir Charles and Lady Cayzer had taken a morning stroll around the grounds of the castle, and he had stopped to talk to his head gamekeeper, Robert Gilchrist, about a hare hunt. Less than an hour later, domestic servants heard two loud shots. Mr Wexham, who had been butler for 11 years, was found lying on the floor of his pantry. On a table near the body was a carafe of water that he had been filling for lunch. Sir Charles was found with a double-barrelled sporting gun between his legs. He had fallen outside the open door of the pantry, close to the castle's gunroom. No letter or note which could shed light on the tragedy was found. A friend of Mrs Wexham's confirmed that the couple's 10-year-old son was being cared for by relatives while she was in Kinpurnie.

Benjamin Wexham had been in Scotland for just five months at the time of the shooting. Lady Cayzer, her husband, their two daughters and young son had been in residence at the castle for some time. Sir Charles, the third baronet, was a director of the shipping company Cayzer, Irvine and Co. Ltd, managers of Clan Line Steamers. His grandfather – founder of the firm – had died in 1916, leaving a fortune of £1,900,000. Sir Charles was reported to have had a nervous breakdown a few months before the shooting, but at the outbreak of war, having been a lieutenant in the 19th Hussars, offered his services to the War

Office and was commissioned. He resigned not long after owing to his health. The *Mirror* wrote that Sir Charles had served with distinction in the First World War and had been wounded. Just a few weeks before the Armistice he was captured by the Germans.

Although the newspapers didn't really confirm what happened and reports are sketchy, the inference was that Sir Charles shot his butler before shooting himself.

# The Death of George Kerr

1940

George Kerr, a disabled ex-soldier, vanished in February 1940. His bloodstained car was found on a lonely marsh road between Pevensey and Bexhill, East Sussex. He was known to have two obsessions – a great fear of car thieves and a dread of the black-out. These facts were released on 29th February after police had searched the marshes and dragged the waterways near where the car was found. They were not ruling out the possibility that George, who ran a car hire business, had been murdered. He was known to carry fairly large sums of money, and it was believed he might have been attacked and robbed. On the floor and front seat of his car, which was found with all the lights on at 4.30pm, there were pools of blood. After losing so much blood and already suffering from war injuries – he had had an operation on his foot just a year before – police were asking how he had left the car unaided.

George hadn't been seen since 7.00am on the day he went missing from his lodgings in Cambridge Road, Hastings. He was 49 and had been widowed for seven years. The police tried to check whether George had arranged to meet a fare. He had such a fear of car thieves that he had fitted a secret ignition device. "The ordinary ignition switch on Kerr's car was only a dummy," a member of his garage staff said. "If a stranger switched it on the car would not start. Kerr had had a secret switch fitted right under the cowling near the steering column, and unless this was pushed forward the car would not start."

Just a little later on the day on which George's disappearance was reported in the *Mirror*, his body was found about a mile from the car in a stream. No one really knows what happened to the "smiling man".

# Fire Death Mystery in Peterborough

## 1940

Scotland Yard detectives travelled to Peterborough at the end of February 1940 to investigate the death of Grace Elizabeth Hadman, who was found dead after a fire at her cottage. When a doctor examined her charred body he found that she had a massive head wound. Grace lived with her husband and four children in the cottage in Lower Lodge, Chesterton. On the morning of the fire her husband got up for work at 4.00am, lit the fire, took her a cup of tea and then left. Shortly afterwards, his brother, who lived next door, heard the children screaming. He jumped out of bed and saw dense clouds of smoke coming from the cottage, so he rushed out and rescued the children, aged nine, eight, four and 11 months, and sent for the fire brigade. His brother was later reported in the press to have also been present. Firemen found the children's mother's charred remains.

The pathologist was expected to disclose that Grace had been "alive, but only just" when the fire broke out. When the inquest was opened on 1st March 1940, Scotland Yard officers and a police photographer were continuing their investigation at the house, and two suitcases containing debris had been removed for further examination. Charles Hadman, the victim's husband, and his brother William were said to have been beaten back by flames when they tried to find Elizabeth. The district coroner, Major S.G. Cook, opened the inquest at Norman Cross, Huntingdon after taking formal evidence of identification from Charles Hadman, a farm labourer. He said: "There is considerable doubt apparently as to what was the cause of death so I am going to adjourn the inquest for further inquiries. I perhaps might say what I think is generally known that I ordered a post mortem examination ... I have no report on that yet." Charles Hadman told the *Mirror*: "I left home to go to work about 100 yards away at about 4.30am on Wednesday morning. I had been gone about twenty minutes or so when I heard my brother, William, who lives next door with my mother, shouting.

"I went back to see what was the matter. I helped my brother to get the children out safely. Then I went back upstairs for my wife, but couldn't find her. I got into the living room downstairs through a window. Someone threw water through the pantry window and drove the flames over to me. I could not find her there."

Police believed that Mrs Hadman had been murdered and on 4th March were expected to make an arrest imminently. An exhaustive search had been made for the murder weapon – probably a hatchet or axe – which inflicted a near-fatal blow. Chief Inspector Walter Bridger from Scotland Yard, who was in charge of the investigation, had been trying to establish what the victim had been doing the evening before her murder. The children, by this point, were reported to be staying with their grandmother in Peterborough. Only the nine-year-old knew that their mother was dead.

While he was milking cows in the shed with his brother, Arthur Charles Hadman was arrested on 4th March by detectives from Scotland Yard and charged at Stangrounds police station with the murder of his wife. He was expected to be brought before a special court at Old Fletton on 5th March. The officers who accompanied him to the station included Chief Inspector Bridger and Sergeant Marshall – both from Scotland Yard – alongside Superintendent Hodson of Huntingdon police and Patrol Driver

Douglas. Hadman was dressed for work at the time of the arrest, so Douglas was sent to the house to retrieve his coat.

One month later, Hadman's nine-year-old daughter went into the witness box to tell the court about her father. He sat and watched his child as she said that the morning her mother was found dead he had wakened her and asked: "Are you all right?" Kathleen Hadman told the court that her mother had left the family home at around 7.30pm the night before the fire, which was the last time she had seen her. Asked what her father did on the fateful day, she said: "He went downstairs. After he went down I smelt smoke. I got out of bed and saw downstairs was all smoke. I looked in Mummy's room and she wasn't there. I shouted out of the window, and Uncle Bill spoke to me and told me to call my mother, but I said she was not in bed." Defence counsel Mr Pollock asked: "Your father and mother and you and your brothers were a happy family together, weren't you?" The child replied: "Yes."

The fire, the court heard, had been confined to the living room, the door of which was alight. After the flames had been subdued, firemen entered the room but could not find Mrs Hadman. Charles Hadman entered through the living room window and led firemen to the charred remains of his wife. Hadman said in a statement to police that the living room fire was allowed to burn through the night. When he awoke at 4.00am he would put some sticks on the fire to boil a kettle before making a cup of tea. After he arrived at the farm that morning he heard his brother shouting and saw the fire at his home. Someone said they could see something moving in the living room, but Hadman claimed that smoke had prevented him from entering the building again after rescuing his children. "I made a second attempt to get near my wife, who was in a corner of the living room, but was unable to reach her," he stated. Mr Paling said the condition of Mrs Hadman's head wounds showed that they must have been inflicted at least one hour and possibly as much as four hours before the fire started. The court adjourned until Friday 12th April.

When the hearing continued, news reports that added no further details about the murder of Mrs Hadman towards the end of May 1940 were the last mention of the case. However, in further details, it was stated that Hadman had severely injured his wife and poured petrol around the small living room including over her body. He then set the room alight. The pathologist said that Grace had a very thin skull, and would probably have died as the result of a fall; this would have led to her death before the fire was started. Hadman was found guilty of manslaughter on 22nd May 1940 and served seven years in prison.

# Burglary that Led to Murder in Durham

## 1940

Senior officers called on the young widow of Constable William Shiell (28), at her home in Coxhoe, County Durham, on 1st March

1940 to pay their respects. As they left they swore: "We will get the killers." Constable Shiell was fatally shot when he cornered two men after they burgled the local village co-operative in the black-out. The £50 reward offered for the capture of the men was doubled after the PC's death. "A shop breaking instrument, bent in an unusual way, is the latest clue in the murder," wrote the *Mirror* on 4th March. The tool was found by the police at the back of the Coxhoe Co-op, where it had apparently been used to force bolts and bars on doors by pushing it through the letter box. The tool and a bullet taken from the constable's body were the main clues that the police had to go on. The bullet was a .35 calibre, and could have been fired from a known type of German automatic, according to reports.

Funeral arrangements were completed on 3rd March; Constable Shiell's body was to be taken to his home, and from there conveyed with a guard of military police officers six miles through country lanes to Spennymoor. The funeral service was to be held at St Andrew's Church – the church in which the murdered officer had been married five years before. A friend of the family told the *Mirror*: "Mrs Shiell seems to be stunned by the tragedy. They had made so many plans for their future and for their baby daughter. Now Barbara is the only comfort she has."

On 4th March 1940, two men appeared at Durham County Constabulary headquarters charged with the murder of the police officer. Vincent Ostler (24), from Hawksworth near Otley, and William Appleby (27), also from Hawksworth, were the accused.

They were remanded at the request of Superintendent Johnson, who said the two men had been apprehended early that same morning. The arrests followed a night of police activity in the Wharfedale area, involving Durham and West Riding police. Constable Shiell had lived for two days following the shooting, and while on his deathbed made a statement that read: "I chased the men and cornered them. One of them pulled out a revolver and the other said: 'Let him have it. He is all alone.'" At the resumed hearing on 7th March, two young women believed to be the wives of the accused men were in court when the statement was read out.

After a five-day trial, Ostler, a mechanic, and Appleby, who worked as a joiner, were both found guilty of the murder at Leeds Assizes on 10th May 1940. It took the jury two hours to consider their verdict, and they added a rider recommending mercy for Appleby. Both men were sentenced to death.

# Assassin Kills Sir Michael O'Dwyer

1940

Sir Michael O'Dwyer (75), Governor of the Punjab during the Amritsar riots in 1919, was shot dead by a gunman at a crowded meeting in Caxton Hall, Westminster, London on 13th March 1940. The gunman fired first at Lord Zetland, Secretary of State for India, wounding him before turning his gun and shooting and wounding Lord Lamington (79), ex-Governor of Bombay and Sir Louis Dane (84), another ex-Governor of Punjab. Nearly 300 men and women had heard Sir Percy Sykes address the meeting of the East India Association in the Tudor Room. Lord Zetland was in the chair. The meeting was about to close, and Lord Lamington had risen to propose a vote of thanks, when the gunman walked to the press table, pulled out a revolver and began firing. As the first two shots were fired, Lord Zetland toppled over and collapsed on the arms of his chair. Sir Michael O'Dwyer jumped up and two shots entered his heart. He died immediately. The assassin fired six times, and with his last two bullets he wounded Lord Lamington and Sir Louis, who had been sitting at each end of the front row of the audience. Sir Louis was hit in the arm, while Lamington's right hand was shattered. For a shocked second no one moved, then the assassin turned, shouted "Make way, make way," and dashed down the aisle. Two men, one of them in uniform, jumped on the man and detained him. At this point chaos broke out, and Dr Grace McKinnon, a retired Indian medical missionary, hurried forward. She could see immediately that Sir Michael was dead and turned to help those who were wounded. Another doctor was also able to help; Dr Lawrence, brother of Lawrence of Arabia, was also in the audience. Lord Lamington was taken by cab to his home in Wilton Place, while Lady Lionel Jacob who had attended the meeting said: "I was sitting in the third row. I noticed a man sitting a yard or two away.

I said to my neighbour Mr J.F. Sale what a horrible looking man. He was sitting fidgeting and wriggling about. Then I saw him rise, walk forward, draw a revolver with a long barrel from his coat and aim shots in rapid succession at those sitting on the platform."

For more than two hours no one was allowed to leave the hall while 50 Scotland Yard officers took statements from everyone present. Sir Hari Singh Gour, the Indian social reformer and jurist, who was a witness of the assassination, said: "It was a dastardly act. As for Sir Michael's speech, it was not aggressive at all, but a description of the work he had done as Lieutenant-Governor of Punjab." Another member of the audience said: "Lord Zetland was lying sprawled out on the platform and I heard him say to a woman who bent over him: 'Never mind me, I'm all right.' As the people pushed forward it was difficult to see who had been hurt. It appeared to me as though Sir Michael and Sir Louis Dane had attempted to rush at the man to spoil his aim after he had fired the first two shots. Apparently the man did not shout any slogan when he rushed forward but some people say he cried: 'I'm press.'"

Shortly after 7.00pm, Sir Philip Game, Chief Commissioner of the Metropolitan Police, arrived at Caxton Hall to direct the inquiry. As police barricaded the door, people began arriving to attend the annual dance of the Chase National Bank of New York. Sir Michael O'Dwyer and his wife were known to go to the cinema on Wednesday afternoons, but he had decided to attend the meeting instead. "I shall be back at five," he said cheerily to

Gertrude, the couple's maid. She wept as she told the *Mirror*: "Oh, how I wish he had gone to the pictures today." A phone call from Sir Percy Sykes told Lady O'Dwyer that her husband had been seriously wounded. She went to Westminster Hospital, where she discovered he had died at the scene. Lord Zetland told reporters after he was allowed out of hospital: "I felt a sharp pain in my ribs. It rather knocked me out, and while I was lying down I heard some other shooting going on, but did not see what happened. After that I was taken to St George's Hospital and X-rayed and nothing was found to be broken. I do not think I am very much the worse for it, though there are some bad bruises on the ribs. It was found afterwards that it was a bullet which had struck me. There are marks in my clothes where it went through, marks of burning in my jacket, shirt and vest. The bullet was found in my clothes. My ribs are all bandaged up now, so I do not know whether the bullet actually broke the skin."

News of the assassination was broadcast by Germany at 9.15pm. The German announcer commented: "Thus the Indian Freedom Movement proceeded to direct action against the British oppressors."

Sir Percy Sykes gave an interview to the *Mirror*, in which he said that after he had given a lecture at Caxton Hall, which was crowded with around 400 seated and at least another 50 standing, he was followed by Lord Zetland, who spoke for a quarter of an hour. Sir Michael spoke next, for a further 15 minutes, on the importance of Britain remaining friends with

Afghanistan. Then Mrs Malan – better known as Audrey Harris, author of *All Around Asia* – spoke for a short time before Sir Louis gave a few words. Lord Lamington was asked to wind up the meeting. The shots rang out shortly thereafter, and Sir Percy described how Sir Michael fell bleeding to the floor. He said: "I glimpsed the assassin racing away with his revolver still smoking and dashed after him which in the moment of excitement seemed the natural thing to do. Miss Bertha Herring … bravely tried to stop him. Then Mr C.W.H. Riches, who is nearly sixty years old jumped on the assassin and Captain Dunstead, who is a Deputy Commission in India, helped him pinion the man down. Riches wrested the revolver from the man's hand. I quickly went back to the platform and there I saw a terrible sight. Sir Michael was lying there, obviously beyond help and there were three wounded men by him."

He continued that Sir Louis was only slightly injured and was "quite cheerful", but that Lord Lamington, "poor fellow", had a bullet through his hand. Lord Zetland, he said, was lying down looking very ill and for a moment Sir Percy was worried that he too was "dangerously hurt". He stated: "For a moment I felt I was on the battlefield again and was reminded of the last attempt to assassinate me – in that case made by the Germans when I was in command of the troops in Central Persia in 1917."

General Sir Ian Hamilton told the newspaper that the death of Sir Michael was revenge after 20 years. When told of his friend's murder he said: "Well that's the end of the Amritsar episode.

Mark my words, this is no new affair. It is a murder of revenge. Amritsar was never forgotten. Sir Michael came in for particular hatred, for he upheld the action of General Dyer in shooting on the mob. He always held the same view about that affair; that he was right and acted the right way." At Amritsar, Brigadier General Dyer had ordered troops to open fire to disperse a crowd of about 10,000 which had assembled against his orders. Between 200 and 300 people were killed. At an inquiry in 1920 the General was severely censured for his conduct, first because he fired without warning and second because he continued firing for too long. He was deprived of his command.

Meanwhile, Bertha Herring, a member of the Royal Central Asian Society, had gone to hear her friend Sir Percy speak at the meeting. She told the *Mirror*: "At the end of the lecture, I was standing in the gangway preparing to leave the hall when I heard three shots. At first I thought they were IRA explosions, but when I turned round I saw a man running down the passage with a smoking revolver in his hand. There were two men standing close to me, and we all rushed at once to stop the assassin. He struggled to get free and I found myself on the floor. When I got free I saw someone had pinioned him down by throwing a coat over him so I went up on to the platform to see if I could render first aid. To my horror Sir Michael O'Dwyer was obviously beyond help. I was able to make the other injured men more comfortable until the doctors arrived."

Smiling broadly, Mahomed Singh Azad (37) made a three-minute appearance at Bow Street police court on 14th March 1940, accused of the murder of Sir Michael. The police alleged he told them: "I just meant to protest." He was remanded for a week. The court was strongly guarded and Detective Inspector Swain was the only witness. As the prisoner watched him with a grin, the senior officer said: "I saw the body of Sir Michael O'Dwyer in a room at Caxton Hall last night. Later I saw the prisoner and said: 'I am going to take you to Cannon Row police station, where you will be charged with the murder of Sir Michael O'Dwyer.' He said: 'I'll tell you how I made a protest.' At the police station he made a statement. He was charged with the murder, cautioned and said: 'I did not mean to kill him … I did not mean to kill anybody.'" On the charge sheet, Azad was described as an engineer living in Mornington Crescent, London.

In mid-March, one of two bullets which caused the death of Sir Michael was produced at the inquest in Westminster. Sir Bernard Spilsbury, the pathologist, described how he had found the bullet in the body. The second bullet was not found in the body. The cause of death was haemorrhage from two wounds. The inquest was then adjourned until 8th May, pending completion of criminal proceedings against Azad. As he was led in and out of the hearing, he smiled broadly again.

The following month, as evidence was given at Bow Street police court, Azad said: "I don't mind dying. What is the use of waiting till you get old? That is not good. You want to die when you are young. That is good. That is what I am doing … I am dying for my country." Detective Inspector Dayton said that in Azad's possession was a red diary for 1940, and on the page headed "Cash Account, December 1940" was written "Sir Michael O'Dwyer, Sunnybank, Selsdon, South Devon." At the accused's home address detectives had found a small black diary for 1939 where the same message was written. Detective Sergeant Jones gave evidence of statements alleged to have been made by Azad. One read: "I did it because I had a grudge against him. He deserved it." He also asked: "Is Zetland dead? He ought to be ..." Robert Churchill, a gun expert, said the ammunition handed to him by the police was old, possibly around 30 years old. The blackening around the two bullet holes in Sir Michael's jacket proved that the weapon had been held at close range – less than 9in away. Pleading not guilty and reserving his defence, Azad was remanded until 2nd April for formal committal to the Old Bailey.

The engineer thumped his clenched fist on the dock rail and spat into the court as he was sentenced to death at the Old Bailey on 5th June 1940. He had insisted the shooting was an accident, and was also reported to have been on hunger strike while in custody.

On 28th June, Bertha Herring was awarded an MBE for her part in trying to apprehend the assassin at Caxton Hall; she was described as having undertaken "a very brave act". She had seized Azad as hard as she could as he tried to escape, and had tried to grapple with him before he flung her back.

# The Girl in the Wardrobe

## 1940

The body of a girl in her early twenties was found in a locked wardrobe when police searched a house in one of the back streets of Brighton at the very end of February 1940. The young woman, who was partly undressed, wasn't identified immediately, and police were unsure how long she had been dead. Brighton's police asked for the services of Sir Bernard Spilsbury, the pathologist, and a woman visited the local police station to give a long statement to detectives. She was charged and detained, due to appear in court on 1st March.

Brighton police appealed for help in identifying the girl whose body had been found, and issued the following description: "About twenty-five, 5ft, 3½ inches in height with fair or light brown hair, blue eyes, short nose inclined to turn up, good natural teeth, rather large but not prominent, and small feet and hands. She may possibly have worn tortoise-shell spectacles and there is a white bone bangle on the left arm. She wore a wine-coloured coat."

Scotland Yard were also called in, and Sir Bernard examined the body. Police Sergeant Collyer stated at the police court earlier in the day that he had found the body in a locked wardrobe of a bedroom in the house, which belonged to Hilda Mary Morgan, in Castle Street. Charges were made against Morgan (46) and

Home Front Killers

Samuel Weitzman (37), from Offington Lane, Worthing. They were accused of conspiring to procure an operation on Rosaline Walsh. Collyer confirmed that Morgan had made a statement at Brighton police station, then Weitzman had been collected from Worthing and the couple were now being charged. Weitzman replied: "I have never seen the woman before." Both were then held on remand. Weitzman was granted bail, but Superintendent Pelling said that another serious charge might be brought against Morgan.

When Constance Cowan Ison (30), daughter of an affluent retired manufacturer's agent, visited her parents' home in Park Hill, Clapham, London for Christmas 1939 she didn't appear to have a care in the world. She told her family how happy she was in her job as a masseuse at Brighton Municipal Hospital, where she had been employed for some time. The attractive, fair-haired, blue-eyed woman was always fashionably dressed and described as one of the most popular woman at the hospital. On 4th March 1940, Mr and Mrs Ison learned that their daughter was dead. She was identified by the bone bangle as the girl whose body was found in the locked wardrobe. The couple travelled to Brighton hoping against hope that there had been some terrible mistake, but they finally established the identity of the dead woman. William Ison, the brother of the victim, was working in his office at a London brewery when he received the news by phone. "I have not seen Connie since Christmas," he told the *Mirror* sadly. "We never dreamed she was in trouble. Connie had one or two men friends, but she was not engaged so far as we knew. This has been a terrible shock." Miss Ison, who trained as a masseuse in Yorkshire, had been away from home for several years, and only managed to get home during holiday periods when work commitments allowed. She was known to have been lodging in Marine Gardens in Brighton at the time of her death.

Two days later, it was revealed that shock following an injection was what had killed her. Evidence was given by Dr L.R. Janes, a pathologist at the Royal Sussex County Hospital at the inquest in Brighton on 6th March. The inquest was adjourned. Three days later, Pelling applied for a witness summons for the Brighton Postmaster to produce two telegrams said to concern the case. Hilda Morgan was to be remanded until 18th March accused of murdering Connie Cowan Ison. She was also accused with Weitzman of conspiring with intent to procure the miscarriage of Rosaline Walsh between 19th and 29th February 1940. Morgan's defence counsel was confirmed as Mr S.W.A. Cushman.

On 18th March Mr G.R. Paling opened the prosecution's case with the words: "She has certainly killed two women and very nearly killed another." He continued: "In the submission of the prosecution she is nothing more than a professional abortionist." Seven additional charges were preferred against the accused woman, who described herself as a housekeeper. The additional charges related to the alleged unlawful use of an instrument on four other women. Weitzman also appeared in the dock that day, charged with conspiring to procure miscarriage on Rosaline Walsh from Worthing. Mr Paling said that in January 1940 Miss Walsh had become pregnant. Weitzman had driven her to Brighton, where she had seen Morgan, who said she could help. A fee of £4 was agreed. Hearing that the police were making inquiries, Miss Walsh, advised by Weitzman, postponed a further visit to Morgan. In a statement he denied he knew why Rosaline Walsh was visiting the accused. He denied knowing Morgan and said he had wanted nothing to do with an abortion. When police searched Morgan's premises they had discovered the body of Connie. In an alleged statement, Morgan claimed that the young woman had become ill and she had done her best to look after her. The statement added: "The next thing I remember was a knock at the door. It was a telegram from Mr Wootton [a seaman with whom the accused was living] to say he was coming home. I thought it was a very nice homecoming for a man after being at sea for about four months. I dragged her into the back room. She was dead then … Later I put the body into the wardrobe and locked it."

Mr Paling said that Connie Ison was not the first girl to die suddenly in Morgan's home. On 18th May 1939 police had found a 24-year-old girl dead in bed following a premature birth. There were no further news reports on the story.

# Howard Dudley Stone
1940

A youth of 19 who, it was said, had developed a great hatred of Germans was charged at Ealing on 24th June 1940 with the murder of his 18-year-old cousin, whose father was German. Howard Stone, a clerk from Hamilton Road, Ealing was formally remanded for a week to be committed for trial, charged with the murder of Leslie Wilkesman from Western Gardens, Ealing. Vincent Evans, prosecuting, said the two youths had been brought up more like brothers than cousins. However, on the evening of 7th June, Wilkesman was talking to two neighbours when Stone approached with a gun. He fired at his cousin, who fell wounded in the face. He died on arrival at hospital. The following night, Stone surrendered at a police station. He made a written statement: "I was anxious about the war. I felt the Germans are such devilish psychologists. I felt that Bunty [the name by which Leslie was known] was turning against my family. I decided to kill him."

Harold Henry Stone, a company director, confirmed that he was the accused's father and uncle of the murdered teenager. He said that Bunty's father was in Germany and that he and Stone had always been great friends. He said his son had been "strange in his manner" and had threatened to take his life. He identified two letters in his son's handwriting. One read: "Possibly you wonder how I got like this. I was brought up with a German boy. Never weaken before the Germans." Mr Stone said that his son had developed a great hatred of Germany. Once when he was talking of Nazi atrocities, his son had "blazed up" and said: "Why did you let me be brought up with a German boy?" As with many wartime news reports, there were no follow-up articles giving a conclusion to the story.

# Julia Ransom

## 1940

An arrest was expected imminently on 12th July 1940 in connection with the murder of three women found at a lonely farmhouse in Crittenden in Matfield, near Tonbridge in Kent. The scene of the crime was reconstructed by four police officers in a further hunt for clues. Chief Inspector Beveridge from Scotland Yard, together with Inspector Cherrill, a fingerprints expert, and other CID officers, watched the experiment and timed the proceedings. A few miles away in the mortuary at Pembury, Sir Bernard Spilsbury carried out a three-hour post-mortem examination, which proved that all three women had been shot and one had also been bludgeoned. The victims were Dorothy Fisher (45), her daughter Freda Fisher (20) and their housekeeper, Charlotte Saunders (37). After the reconstruction, Chief Inspector Beveridge met Mr Fisher, Dorothy's widower.

Later, police found the gun that they suspected had killed all three women. There were indications that more than three shots had been fired at the victims, and inquiries were concentrated at railway stations in the Tonbridge area and at an Oxfordshire railway station which only ran three trains a day. It was understood that an identification parade would be held on 15th July – and a woman who had accompanied police officers from London to Tonbridge was questioned in the hope that she could help with inquiries.

At the identification parade, a number of women all wearing slacks of a similar colour were paraded at Tonbridge police station while four witnesses looked on. Among the women was Julia Ransom (34), who following the parade was charged with the murder of the three women. Ransom's address was given as Carramore Farm, Piddington, near Bicester, Oxfordshire.

Ransom was brought before magistrates at Tonbridge police court. At the inquest on the three victims it was stated that they had been killed by six shots from a shotgun at close range. Two shots, it was said, had killed Mrs Fisher, three had killed her daughter and one had killed Miss Saunders. Evidence of identification was given by Walter Lawrence Fisher, husband of Dorothy. The coroner said that as a person had been arrested and charged with the murders, he would adjourn the inquest until after the court proceedings had been completed, and it was adjourned until 30th September 1940. Ransom was remanded until 30th July, having sat throughout the short hearing on 16th July with her head against the waist of a woman police official, who supported her with her arms round her shoulders in the dock. Detective Inspector Smeed said: "At 3.00pm yesterday, with Chief Inspector Beveridge of the Metropolitan Police, I saw the prisoner to Tonbridge police station. We were both known to her. I said to her: 'On the night of July 9 at Crittenden, Matfield, I saw the bodies of Dorothy Fisher, Freda Fisher and Charlotte Saunders. As the result of inquiries I am now going to charge you with murdering these women.' I cautioned her and she said: 'I didn't do it.'" The inspector added that when he formally charged her with the murder of Dorothy she replied: "I didn't do it. I didn't do it. How could I?" When he charged her with the murder of Freda Fisher she replied: "No, no," but made no reply when charged with the murder of Charlotte. Superintendent W.C. Cook from Tonbridge asked on the evidence for a remand. Ransom confirmed that she didn't want to ask any questions at that stage, and had nothing to say with regard to the application for remand. She was helped from the dock and walked slowly from the court.

Florence Iris Ouida Ransom was said to have committed the crimes while on a "friendly visit" to the wife of her lover, Walter Lawrence Fisher. It was revealed that Dorothy Fisher also had a lover, and he was on friendly terms with her husband. The court heard how crockery had been pieced together to show that Miss Saunders had been preparing tea for four when she was shot through the head. Mr G.R. Paling for the Director of Public Prosecutions said that the Fishers' marriage was not perhaps a happy one. He said: "Mrs Fisher became acquainted with a gentleman of Danish nationality and they became lovers. Mr Fisher took no legal steps to remedy this state of affairs and apparently he was content because he continued to live in the same house with his wife." Mr Paling explained that Mr Fisher used the property at Matfield as a weekend residence. He had become acquainted with Ransom in 1934 after she was widowed. She accompanied him to the Fishers' farm at the weekend and became a frequent visitor, as did Dorothy Fisher's Danish lover. "It was an unusual position," said Mr Paling. "There was a man and wife living under the same roof and each had taken to themselves a lover known to each other and the lovers used to visit their house, but it is not for me in any way to criticize how people lead their lives." In 1938 Fisher bought the farm in Bicester, and gave up his other house in Twickenham in March 1940. In Bicester, Ransom was known as Mrs Fisher. She acted as a sort of secretary/manager to Fisher, running the farm for him while he travelled daily to and from London, and even moved her family into the Bicester farm as domestic servants to help her. Her mother, Mary Guildford, acted as a servant, Frederick Guildford, her brother, was the cowman and his wife Jessie was the dairymaid. They lived in a cottage close to the farm. "The Danish gentleman was eager to live at Crittenden and Mrs Fisher was eager to have him with her," said Paling. "Crittenden, however, is situated in a prohibited area and being an alien he had to obtain police permission to enter the district, but he failed to do so. Mr Fisher was anxious to help his wife and lover so that they could live together, and on July 3 he and Mrs Ransom visited Mrs Fisher at Crittenden and went to police headquarters at Maidstone to try to obtain the necessary permission."

Their attempts to help failed, and that was the last time Fisher saw his wife alive. After describing how the bodies were discovered, Paling said that police officers found a tea tray lying on the floor of the kitchen among some broken crockery. The position of the crockery indicated what Charlotte had been doing before she was shot dead. Superficially it appeared that the motive for the crime was robbery, but that seemed very unlikely, as £15 was found in the farmhouse, together with jewellery. Sir Bernard Spilsbury had found that the wounds were all inflicted from close quarters and the position of the wounds and of the bodies, together with the fact that preparations had been made for tea for four, indicated without doubt that the assailant was known to the three victims.

On the day of the murders, Fisher was in London, and returned to the Bicester farm at around 6.45pm. Ransom did not arrive home until around 9.00pm. She made a statement to police denying that she was at Matfield that day, and asserted that at the time she was alleged to have committed murder she was resting at the Guildfords' cottage, where she was recovering after a fall. Giving his reconstruction of the crime, Paling alleged that it was deliberately planned, and that Ransom had gone to Kent with the gun wrapped in a parcel. At the cottage, where she was received as a friend, it was suggested that she persuaded Freda to walk in front of her and then shot the young woman at close range. She then shot Mrs Fisher, who had probably heard the shots and run in to see what was happening. She too was shot in the back as she tried to run away. Freda then received two more bullets before Charlotte was shot, as the only witness to the other murders. A glove found near one of the bodies was identified as Ransom's. The prosecution alleged that Ransom had asked her brother to show her how the gun worked; he then held it up in court. She had told her brother she wanted to shoot rabbits, but a few days later, when he pestered her to return the gun, he noticed that six cartridges were missing. Ransom said that she was so scared that she had thrown them away. She was then identified by railway officials as being a passenger on the 8.56am train to Bicester on 9th July. Mr Paling went on to state that letters found in Ransom's possession and others found in Kent showed that the accused was jealous of Dorothy Fisher. "Her jealousy extended to opening secretly any letter that Mrs Fisher might write to her husband." Alleging that the Guildfords did not support her alibi, he suggested that when she told the police the false story she had firmly believed her family would support her. "Inquiries made by the police revealed that Mrs Guildford is the prisoner's mother and that Fred Guildford, the cowman, is her brother ... and that for some reason best known to herself she concealed that relationship from Mr Fisher and induced her family also to conceal it." While Fisher was giving the first part of his evidence, Ransom covered her ears with her hands and sobbed.

Fisher said that his wife was in love with the Danish Mr Westergaurd, and that he didn't know until the death of his wife that Mrs Guildford was his lover's mother. Mrs Guildford broke down in the witness box as she said she hadn't seen her daughter all day on 9th July until 9.00pm. She also said her daughter had asked her not to let Fisher know she had been out all day. Fred

Guildford identified the gun used in the murders as his own, and confirmed that he had shown his sister how to use it the day before the deaths. Jessie Guildford told the court that she had shown Ransom a newspaper report about the murders. "Mrs Ransom was in her bedroom at the time," she said. "She cried out ... She staggered and I helped her to the bed." Jessie also admitted that she hadn't been entirely truthful with the police when they first came to question Ransom. She said that Ransom had told her the police were after her, and she wanted the young woman to shield her. Mrs Guildford senior was then recalled to the witness box, and said that at breakfast time on 9th July her son had brought her a note from Ransom. It had since been destroyed, but she said it was in her daughter's handwriting and read: "Mrs G. will you come down and see to Mr Fisher and the farm and don't let anybody on the farm know I am out. Burn this."

On 14th August 1940 a baker's driver told the inquest that he had driven the accused from near the scene of the murders. He had then picked out Ransom at the police identity parade. William Playfoot had been loading the baker's van on the Matfield road, and was approached by Ransom who was looking for a quick lift to Tonbridge. He stated that she had a long parcel wrapped in brown paper.

Ransom was committed for trial at the Old Bailey. She pleaded not guilty and reserved her defence. Meanwhile, Detective Sergeant F.K. Smith said that in a bureau at the cottage a number of letters had been found. One letter, from Julia, was addressed to: "My dear Freda. You will remember your little outburst on the Saturday morning before your departure [Freda had stayed with Ransom and her father for two weeks in June]. Owing to that Daddy and I had a good talk about you in the evening and it was then we made our decision ... I can assure you once again that we were fully agreed that you should not come again." The letter concluded: "Lots of love from Julia." In Ransom's bag, police found a letter from Freda dated just a day later, on 15<sup>th</sup> June. It read: "Thanking Julia for her nice long letter. As you still say that you and daddy have agreed it is best for me not to come to Carramore again, even after my letters to both of you saying I would like to come again. I feel I must have offended you. This I had not meant to do and I am sorry. Anyway I think it was rather silly of daddy to say when in the car with me that I could come when I liked. But as he has so many more important things to think about, perhaps it was easier for him just to say that and I don't blame him. You say you are mystified. I am too, and cannot understand why there has been all this trouble. Mummie thanks you for her letter."

The court at the Old Bailey heard on 23<sup>rd</sup> September that Ransom – it was suggested – suffered from lapses in memory, and the defence successfully made an application for her trial to be postponed until the following sessions. Mr Stuart Horner, defending, said he made the application so that Ransom could be examined by an independent neurologist to find out her medical history. Mr Justice Hallett said: "Hysteria and a desire for publicity or what?" to which Horner replied: "No. Lapses of memory which may be due to a basic source."

On 8th November 1940 Ransom sat in tears facing her mother in the witness box in court number one at the Old Bailey. It was day two of Ransom's trial for triple murder. Mrs Guildford was asked by counsel for the defence if she remembered the day her daughter was born 35 years earlier. She too had tears streaming down her cheeks. In a quiet voice she told the hushed court of her daughter's early life and her life as a young woman. When asked on the day of the murders where she had been for so many hours, Ransom had told her mother that she had been chasing a cat and that she had fallen and hit her head on a rock, which rendered her unconscious for quite some time. The following day she told her mother that she had actually been out with another man – named Dudley – but that she didn't want Fisher to know as he wouldn't have understood.

On 11th November Ransom entered the witness box and shocked the court with five soft words. When asked if Mrs Guildford was her mother, she replied: "I have never believed that." There was a moment's silence, and then no further reference was made to the dramatic denial. During cross-examination, Ransom was closely questioned about the man known only as Dudley. She said she had known a man by that name many years before but believed he was now dead. St John Hutchinson, prosecuting, asked her if she had seen another man of the same name in July 1940. Ransom said she didn't think so. Mr Hutchinson told her that Dr Dudley Benjafield had a Harley Street address. She then told the judge that he was a specialist she thought she had seen some years before. Asked if she had seen Dr Benjafield in July and whether she had written to him on 3rd July Ransom replied that she didn't think she had. Mr Hutchinson then produced a letter, which he handed in as an exhibit. Ransom was asked to read the letter, and then confirmed that she had written it; prosecuting counsel said he was glad her memory was getting better. She then told the court that when she had seen Dr Benjafield on 12th July it wasn't a professional visit.

It took the jury just 47 minutes on 12th November after a four-day trial to find Ransom guilty of murder. When the guilty verdict was read out, she slumped forward after protesting her innocence. As the black cap was placed on the judge's head she gave a low moan and slouched lower in the arms of her warders. The judge spoke the sentence rapidly, and only when he had finished speaking did he look at the condemned woman, whose moans were audible above his grim words. She was carried sobbing from the dock, just a few feet from the bowed figure of her former lover Walter Fisher. Mrs Guildford cried after the trial ended that her heart was breaking. She told reporters that she could never believe that a child of hers could do "that dreadful thing". Talking to the *Mirror* following the verdict, Fisher said: "This terrible business has been a nightmare. That ghastly scene in the dock will stay with me always. Mrs Ransom is a remarkable woman of great charm and we were very happy together … I cannot understand her denial that Mrs Guildford was her mother. She used to make something of a mystery about her parents, and the suggestion she used to make was that she was in some way related to a titled family."

Ransom appeared white-faced at the Court of Criminal Appeal in London on 9th December 1940. She had been found guilty only of the murder of Dorothy Fisher. While the prosecution alleged that she had also murdered Freda and Charlotte, eventually no charges with regard to those deaths were brought by the Crown. Her appeal failed, and as she heard the court's decision she sank back into her chair and rocked forwards and backwards. The Lord Chief Justice quietly said: "The verdict of jury cannot be disturbed." He lowered his eyes to his desk, and apart from when Ransom appeared before them, none of the three judges looked at the condemned woman. The *Mirror* wrote: "Mrs Ransom, helped to her feet, gazed wildly round the court before she was led away – to pay the penalty for one of the most coldly executed crimes of recent years." On the orders of the Home Secretary a medical inquiry was directed into Ransom's health. She was certified insane and the sentence of death was respited. The Home Secretary ordered that Ransom be removed to Broadmoor.

# Stanley Edward Cole

1940

The young wife of a former postman – then serving in the army – was found dead early on 23rd August 1940 in the kitchen of her home in Hartfield Crescent, Wimbledon, London. Her nine-year-old daughter remained asleep upstairs in bed. Later that same day, Wimbledon magistrates remanded Stanley Cole (23), a wood machinist, who was alleged to have admitted that he murdered Doris Girl (29). Detective Inspector Francis Gillan said he had interviewed Cole at the police station and told him: "I understand you have called here in connection with her death." The inspector continued: "He said: 'She is dead, then?'" He then confirmed that the accused had little more to say. Cole made a statement that he then signed in Gillan's presence.

Homeless Cole was sent for trial at the Old Bailey on 30th August for the murder of Mrs Girl, who was found dead with a stab wound in her back. Vincent Evans, prosecuting, told the Wimbledon hearing that Mrs Girl and Cole were on quite friendly terms, and that the Crown had no known motive for the murder. The prosecution stated that when Mr Girl was away on active service, there was evidence to suggest that Cole stayed at their family home on a sofa in the kitchen. At about 12.40am on 23rd August, Cole staggered up against the door at Wimbledon police station and said: "I've killed a woman at Hartfield Crescent." He began to sob and said: "I stabbed her in the back. Why did I do it?" When police went to the house they found Doris lying on her back on the floor – a carving knife still in the wound. In a statement Cole said: "I picked up a knife from the table and stabbed her in the back. It ran through her like running through butter." There was evidence, according to the prosecution, of quarrels, but there was nothing to suggest that they had had an argument that night. There was no sign of a struggle, and Cole appeared to have stabbed Doris without warning.

On 12th September 1940, Cole was found guilty of murder at the Old Bailey and sentenced to death. Cole had pleaded not guilty, but did not go into the witness box. His appeal against the death sentence failed on 15th October in the Court of Appeal. He was executed on 31st October.

# The Murder of Jean Brown
## 1940

Sirens were sounding the "All Clear" as Jean Brown (23) lay murdered in her basement flat in Plymouth, Devon. People sitting on the stairs above heard nothing. The dead woman was discovered by a man who lived in another flat, lying fully clothed on the floor near her bed. She had been strangled. Deputy Chief Constable W.T. Hutchings, together with other CID officers, searched all night for clues. The unmarried woman had lived in the flat for two years, and was known as "Blondie Strange". Her two-year-old daughter Pamela was said to be staying with relatives in the city. On the night she died, Jean had been in a local pub, which she left at 10.15pm with a sailor. Police visited barracks, questioning men who were known to have been close by the flat.

A friend said: "Jean was with me till she left the public house. Shortly before the 'All Clear' sounded she got up to leave with a sailor. As she went past the door two other sailors said something and one stroked her hair. The sailor with her seemed to object to this and told the two others to come outside. All of them went into the passage and soon afterwards Jean came back. She said there was going to be a fight and she wanted to go home. She went back into the passage and did not return." Before she left for the final time, Jean told a barmaid that she was afraid to go home in the dark because there were so many "roughs" in the streets. Police were trying to trace her movements from the time she was seen leaving the pub to the time she died – which was only 10 minutes, according to the police surgeon's estimate: the flat was just 300 yards from the pub. Elizabeth Guildford, who lived in the flat above Jean, said: "I was sitting on the stairs during the raid alarm and heard no one go into the flat below." Meanwhile, police confirmed that they had detained a man.

On 26th September 1940 evidence about the times the air raid sirens were sounded was given at the inquest into the death of Beatrice Loveday "Jean" Brown. In the dock, accused of murdering her with a silk stocking, was Reginald Guy Strange (24), from Raleigh Street, Plymouth. Gordon Clark, for the Director of Public Prosecutions, said that the woman was known as Jean Brown and lived with Strange. A comparison between times and the movements of Jean and those of Strange made him the only possible person to have been on the spot at the time of her death. A note from Brown to Strange which seemed to anticipate a separation between them had been found in the flat. Strange had tried to concoct a story about a man in a sports jacket calling at the premises, but the prosecution said that the "man" was non-existent. Strange had also told an officer: "She had a garter and silk stocking round her neck. I cut the stocking with a knife and took the garter off." Mr Clark said it was significant that when Jean was found her hair was carefully brushed and the clips were all in position. The garter was so small that it would be impossible to put it round her neck without disarranging the hair. Two stockings were found on the floor close to the body. "It looks as though whoever used one or both of these stockings", said Mr Clark, "did so with the hands and not by tying a knot. There was no mark at all at the back of the neck, and it appears that death was due to garroting."

Jean had arrived at the pub at 7.00pm and left three and a quarter hours later while the air raid warning was on. Her body was found at 11.10pm. Strange was known to be in another pub playing darts with William Conway until 10.30pm. He left, and was served chips by John Mignanelli in King Street at 10.35pm. Kathleen Riggs in Well Street spoke to him close to the flat at around 10.45pm. In an alleged statement read in court, Strange said: "Jean had told me about a man who was jealous of her and used to resent her talking to other men ... I don't think she was afraid of him but regarded him as a nuisance. I had never seen the man, but to judge from Jean's conversation he was an oldish man."

As with many stories printed in the war years, no further reports about Jean's death were made.

# The Murder of Mary Hagan

1940

Fifteen-year-old Mary Hagan, a Liverpool schoolgirl, was found dead in a road blockhouse (a type of army barracks) just before midnight, just hours after she left home to buy a newspaper. Neighbours who organized a search party discovered her with head injuries and a bruised throat, while her clothing was muddy and disarranged. On 3rd November 1940, detectives with police dogs searched for clues near the blockhouse. They were particularly anxious to interview an elderly man described as having a "slouching walk" who had been seen in the area, as they believed he could help them trace the murderer. Several people had already been interviewed, and it was established that Mary had gone to three shops near her home. Mary was a popular teenager. She was kind to the more elderly residents in her local area and good with children. Numb with grief, Mrs Hagan spoke of the tragedy from her home in Brookside Avenue, Waterloo, Liverpool. "I sent Mary out about a quarter to seven to get an evening paper. When she did not return within half an hour I grew alarmed. I felt instinctively – I suppose it was a mother's intuition – that something dreadful had happened to her. Neighbours organized a search party of their own when they realized how worried I was."

Despite his prosthetic leg and fear of falling over in the black-out, Mr Hagan, a timekeeper at the docks, joined in the search. "We left our other child John, aged eleven, in the house in case Mary returned," he said. "She was a most cheery and normal girl, always laughing and joking. She was to start a week's holiday and had been planning that very evening what she was going to do with it." Mary was 5ft 4in tall and "well built". She was wearing a three-quarter-length rust brown coat with fur-trimmed collar, white woollen gloves, a pale blue knitted jumper and brown shoes. Her identity disc was on her left wrist. Police issued an appeal for information about her movements when the inquest opened on 4th November.

The following day, the *Mirror* reported that police cars had formed a "moving cordon" around the area where Mary had been found strangled. Fifteen detectives, including the chief of the North-Western CID, tramped the district through the drizzling rain continuing their investigation. It was thought that a soldier with an East Lancashire accent might be able to provide more information, and the military police in the district had been invited to co-operate. They were known to be questioning all soldiers in local barracks who had outside passes for the Saturday night on which Mary died. One soldier – who was seen near the blockhouse on several occasions during the week before the murder – was described as being between 25 and 30 with a sallow complexion. He wore battledress, and people who had seen him described him as being untidy. The inquest was adjourned for a month.

It was revealed on 14th November that police wanted to trace the owner of a man's woollen gabardine raincoat that had been found close to the murder scene. A day later police travelled to London to interview a man they thought might be able to help with their inquiries – and he returned with them to Liverpool. On Monday 18th November the *Mirror* reported that a girl of 17 had been found strangled in a yard in the centre of Bolton, Lancashire, two nights before Mary's death. She was the second girl in a fortnight to have been murdered in the same way. In each case, a soldier aged around 25 was wanted by police.

The Bolton teenager was named as Minnie "Peggy" Stott, a grocery shop manager from the town. Both girls were killed on a Saturday night. Minnie had told her mother that she was going to the cinema – and four hours later, also at just before midnight, she was found strangled just off Bradshaw Gate. Minnie was found by a policeman, lying face down on the ground. She had been assaulted and, like the first victim, her clothes were disarranged. A post-mortem showed that the girl had been killed probably by a cord or thin scarf. Her death took place when people were leaving the cinema near the yard, and police were anxious to trace a man who had joined Minnie and her girlfriend in a fish and chip bar beside the local palais de danse at 9.30pm, two nights before Minnie was killed. The man was the same soldier who they were looking for in connection with Mary's murder; he was said to be on leave and due to report back to his unit on 19th November. He had invited the two girls to have a drink with him and they had had a glass of sherry at the local pub, after which he returned them to the palais de danse. The man was also known to have spoken to a woman in Liverpool, and had told her he had been confined to barracks for some time for having been absent. The witness told police that she believed he came from Bury or Burnley.

Samuel Morgan (27), from Seaforth, was accused at Liverpool County Magistrates' Court of assaulting Annie McVittie and stealing her bicycle and bag on 19th November 1940. He was also wanted in connection with the murder of Mary, and was accused of wilful murder. Superintendent Jackson said that Morgan had been detained in London, and had told London police he knew nothing about the attack and had been taken to Seaforth police station on 13th November. Detective Inspector Floyd said that he was then accused of the assault on Annie, which had taken place in early October 1940. Morgan was remanded until 3rd December while instructions from the Director of Public Prosecutions were awaited. On 3rd January 1941 the Liverpool court heard from Mr J.R. Bishop, prosecuting, that Annie, a shorthand typist, was cycling along the towpath of the Leeds and Liverpool canal on 4th October when she had come across the accused. The Irish Guardsman had robbed her of her possessions. Mr Bishop said that in order to escape, Annie suggested Morgan should hold her coat, which was when she made her escape by diving into the canal and swimming to the other side. Morgan pleaded not guilty and reserved his defence, but was committed for trial at the next Liverpool Assizes.

On 8th February 1941 Morgan was found guilty of the murder of Mary Hagan, and was sentenced to death. Before being sentenced he said: "I still say I am an innocent man." It had taken the jury just 55 minutes to convict him, and the trial had lasted a week. In April, the Attorney General refused an application for Morgan to take an appeal to the House of Lords. He was executed on 9th April 1941 in Walton jail, Liverpool.

# The Death of Jackie Buckley

1940

Brighton police decided to call in Sir Bernard Spilsbury on 5th November 1940 to conduct an autopsy on Mrs Jackie Buckley (46), a blonde dancer, who was found dead outside a club in Western Road, Brighton. Jackie was the owner of the club and ran a dance school from the premises. At first it was thought she had fallen from a window of the club, which was on the second floor of a block of luxury flats, onto the flat roof adjoining the building, but new evidence led the police to suspect murder. Medical opinion was that her severe injuries were not caused by a fall. Jackie was known to mix with "the young set" in Brighton and her marriage, the *Mirror* reported, "was dissolved". She was said to have been about to marry for the second time, and had thrown a party at the club to celebrate the forthcoming wedding. Her fiancé, Bryan McCushworth (31), an engineer from Birmingham who visited her at weekends, was not present at the celebrations. The police, meanwhile, were puzzled about the injuries the victim had received, and the inquest due to have opened on 6th November was postponed until Sir Bernard had carried out a post-mortem. Bryan McCushworth told the *Mirror*: "I was not present at the club on Saturday night when the tragedy occurred and therefore I cannot throw any light on Mrs Buckley's death."

On 11th November, it was expected as the inquest opened that Sir Bernard would support the police theory of "foul play". One theory reported to the newspapers was that she had left her flat and been run down by a car and killed – because of the nature of her injuries – and then carried back to the flat and pushed out of the window to give the appearance of suicide. A report by Mr L.R. Janes, the pathologist, indicated that her injuries were not consistent with a fall. Jackie had suffered brain damage and 17 fractured ribs as well as other significant injuries. He said the injuries to the victim's head and chest occurred several minutes before death, while bruising to the limbs was caused at the point of death. "I think it likely," he added, "that the chest injuries were caused by the wheel of a vehicle." The night before she was found dead she had dined with an officer – who had attended the party.

The inquest was adjourned for a month so that police could conduct further investigations. By this time, accidental death and suicide had both been ruled out. Jackie's son, Robert Buckley (20), confirmed that she was divorced from his father, builder's merchant William Buckley. After the inquest was adjourned, Detective Superintendent Pelling told the *Mirror*: "Men friends of Mrs Buckley have been questioned, but we have no suspect in mind at the moment." Statements were taken from many male admirers of the victim, while police worked on the theory that she was attacked at home and then carried to the block of flats and pushed through a narrow window. By 10th December, police were convinced that they knew there were two men connected with the death of the dance instructor. At the reopened inquest the jury decided she was murdered "by some person or persons unknown." Both the men that police suspected had been questioned, but detectives had been unable to "break down" their alibi. A car belonging to one was examined, but no trace of a road accident was found. The other man was suspected of having helped to carry Mrs Buckley while she was unconscious to the flat roof where her body was later discovered. Both men were known to the victim and knew the layout of the building. Police met following the inquest to discuss further action.

Charles Webb, the coroner, said: "Someone must know a good deal more about it but no one has come forward." In his summing-up he said it was a "puzzling case" and that it was hoped that further evidence in time would lead to the truth. Sylvia Burton from

Hove had told the inquest that she and Jackie had been introduced to two Canadian officers at a greyhound meeting. Lance Corporal Leo Robert Evans said he drove the two women back to Mitre House – where Jackie was found – at around 9.30pm. The coroner remained convinced that more than one perpetrator was involved.

There were no more reports in the *Mirror* into the murder of Jackie Buckley, but in 2010, Adrian Buckley, son of William Buckley and his second wife, pieced together the clues and speculated that his father's first wife had been run over in the car park behind the club and then carried upstairs and flung out of the window to make the death appear as suicide. He wrote about the story in his book *A Murder in Brighton*.

# Beauty Queen Found Dead
1941

Sybil Ann Chilvers (25), from Lee-on-the-Solent in Hampshire, a former Norwich beauty queen, was found by police lying dead on her living room floor in March 1941. Her husband, Donald Chilvers (30), was charged with her murder and remanded in custody at Gosport. The couple, along with their eight-year-old son, had just moved from Norwich.

"Sybil has hurt me in every possible way that a woman can hurt a man," said Chilvers in his diary. The words were read at a hearing on 1st May by Mr E.G. Robey, prosecuting counsel. He continued: "I would have forgiven Sybil for everything, but Sybil would not have it that way. A good time for herself was more important to her than anything else. I cannot bear to think of somebody making love to her. Only God, Sybil and myself know what has happened to us young people. God. He does not talk. Sybil is dead and I myself will soon be dead." Counsel said that to his mother, Chilvers wrote: "Sybil has driven me too far at last."

In July the court heard: "I loved her so much. I just could not bear the thought of somebody else making love to her. But that is what happened tonight again; and she said this was going to happen again in future." Chilvers, a fitter, appeared at Hampshire Assizes and was found guilty of stabbing his wife to death after she attended a dance. He was pronounced insane and ordered to be detained during His Majesty's pleasure. Dr Roy Neville Craig, a specialist, said: "In seventeen or eighteen years I don't think I have come across a mental stress of greater degree." Mr Justice Charles, summing up, said it was clear that the wife had been torturing her husband for years.

# Lionel Watson
## 1941

"I found them both dead," Lionel Watson (31) was alleged to have told police when arrested for the murder of his wife and child. At the hearing in Ealing, West London, his wife was named as Phyllis Crocker (32) and his daughter as Eileen Crocker (18 months). Their bodies were found buried in the garden of Watson's home in Goring Way, Greenford, Middlesex in May 1941.

Lady Humphreys, chairman of the magistrates, asked: "Why is the man named Watson and the wife and child Crocker?" Inspector Deighton said that the police didn't know. Watson was then remanded, as the inspector told how he had interviewed the accused at the factory where he worked as a bakelite moulder. When Watson was told that police were inquiring about the death of his wife and child, he said: "I know. Don't show up here. There is no need to hold me. I found them dead." When charged, he replied: "I did not murder my wife and child." The *Mirror* printed a photograph of Eileen as she was at six weeks old – she had been buried in a shallow grave under paving stones in the back garden.

It later transpired that Watson and Phyllis were not married, although they had told neighbours that they were. Watson appeared in the Ealing court again on 11th July, and Mr H.A.K. Morgan, prosecuting, said poisoning was suspected. Watson was already married and had four other children when he moved in with Phyllis and her baby daughter. He had told his lover that he was divorced, and they then went through a "form of marriage".

"They appeared to be happy but at work Watson showed signs of wishing to 'make an acquaintance' of a girl … called Joan Philby. She gave him no encouragement," said Mr Morgan. But later on Watson began taking 17-year-old Joan out. "He gave her clothes and shoes belonging to the dead woman," he continued. "On Sunday, June 15 when the bodies were actually in the garden of the flat, he asked this girl into the flat, enticed her into the bedroom, showed her fur coats and fox furs, which he said belonged to his divorced wife, and asked her if she would have them." Joan refused. Watson wrote to Joan the day before his arrest. It read: "I took to you as soon as I saw you because you [are] a lot different … and I was beginning to love you." Watson was remanded.

On the same page as the article about Watson, the *Mirror* said: "If Britain deluged bombs on Berlin night after night without interruption the war would soon be over." Writing from New York, John Walters said that even light raids would cause widespread terror and that the Germans were desperately trying to build more shelters and move their industry eastwards. He argued that heavier raids would result in a collapse of morale. He wrote: "When I left Germany British raids were becoming heavier daily. The British were using some terrifyingly powerful new bombs. Hamburg is largely in ruins and shipyards are virtually wiped out. One bomb which fell in a Berlin backyard lifted off nearly all the roofs within a mile."

Phyllis Crocker, 32 was found to have traces of cyanide in her body, as did baby Eileen. On 30th July 1941, cyanide was revealed as the cause of death for both mother and baby, according to Dr Roche Lynch, a senior Home Office pathologist, at the resumed inquest in Hayes. The inquest was then adjourned until September. Meanwhile, Lilian Bound confirmed that her daughter had been a witness at the "marriage" of Watson and Phyllis. It transpired in August 1941 that the margarine page was missing from Eileen's ration book. Watson had given the coupons to Joan. Watson pleaded not guilty to murder but was committed for trial.

"The case for the prosecution is that Watson is a poisoner," said Mr McClure at the Old Bailey on 15th September. Counsel said that Watson had committed bigamy when he "married" Phyllis. A neighbour, Mrs Brown, had seen Watson digging in the garden in May. The hearing was then adjourned, before Watson was found guilty on 18th September. He was sentenced to death and his appeal was announced later that same month. Watson was hanged at Pentonville Prison on 12th November 1941.

# The Murders of Mabel Church and Theodora Greenhill

1941

"Whom did nineteen-year-old Mabel Church meet between the time she was last seen alone in a lounge bar and a half-hour later when she was murdered?" asked the *Mirror* in October 1941. Scotland Yard detectives were trying to discover how the girl's naked body had ended up in a bombed and ruined house in Hampstead

Road, northeast London. She was thought to have been killed at 10.00pm: people in nearby houses were convinced that they had heard screams, but at the time took them for children's cries. When Mabel was found on 13th October, her clothes had been ripped off with great force. She had been strangled with a white piece of underwear, tied so tightly that it cut her flesh. A demolition worker found the murdered girl. "I walked into the house and saw through the broken wall a pair of bare feet. I ran for my foreman and we found the body," he told the *Mirror*. It had been carefully laid on the boards that remained in the basement where they had probably dropped through the open joists. In a handbag nearby police found some letters, a gas mask and some clothing.

Mabel lived with her widowed mother in Tufnell Park and was employed as a clerk in Hackney; she was also a voluntary worker at a West End canteen. She had spent the Sunday evening on which she died with a close friend from West Wickham, Vera Whymark. The day before they had been to the theatre and stayed at Vera's parents' home. On Sunday they had gone to the cinema. They said their goodbyes on the platform at Charing Cross station at 9.00pm and Vera took the train home. Mabel had been expected to return to Tufnell Park, but police traced her movements to a pub in northwest London, where she was seen having a snack in the lounge bar by herself at 9.30pm. She was just 10 minutes' walk away from where her body was found half an hour later. Vera's older sister said that they had been friends since childhood. She was said to be absolutely devastated at the loss of her close friend. Vera's sister also told the *Mirror* that Mabel had a boyfriend, known as Don, who was around 30 years old, but that he was away on active service.

On 15th October 1941, the *Mirror* reported that there had been three murders in one week. Late on 14th October an elderly widow had been found dead in a house in Holland Park, West London, and Jack Child (53), a park keeper from Hendon, had been found shot on the Friday before Mabel was murdered. It was thought that the latest victim, Theodora Greenhill (63), might have known her assailant. There were no signs that her ground-floor flat, where she lived with one of her daughters, had been broken into, and police were working on the theory that she had opened the door to someone familiar. A neighbour said: "While one could not call her a recluse, she kept to herself and seldom went out." Meanwhile, in Mabel's case, the police used a new method for taking fingerprints from a dead body – for the first time in criminal history – although the impressions on Mabel's body appeared to have been made by the victim herself.

A day later, it was reported that with the aid of Sir Bernard Spilsbury, Scotland Yard detectives would be using their highest-profile crime experts to solve the three murders. Mrs Greenhill had been strangled in the drawing room of her flat. She had also suffered head injuries. A pyjama cord had been wound around her neck and she appeared to have been hit with a bottle. Rings had been stripped from her fingers and the flat had been ransacked. Witnesses stated that a man, aged about 60, had been seen leaving the house. He had asked a workman to call him a taxi, into which he had thrown a small trunk and attaché case. He had asked the driver to take him to King's Cross as fast as he could. A missing travelling trunk with the initials A.G. was thought to be a vital clue. Detectives investigating Mabel's death were working on the theory that she had been killed by a motorist and then taken to the house. No other clues had yet been found by detectives hunting the killer of Jack Child.

On 17th October the *Mirror* revealed that Mabel was known to have had secret male friends. Scotland Yard discovered that one of her intimate acquaintances was a married man with a family who had been living apart from his wife; he was now in the army. Though friends described Mabel as "quiet and reserved", she was well known at a number of public houses in northwest London, police established. It was thought that jealousy could have been the motive for her murder. Police wanted to interview a soldier, they revealed, as the inquest opened at St Pancras. It was then adjourned. Police also hoped that a man and woman who were in Mote Mount Park, Hendon, on the day Jack Child was shot might be able to provide them with more details.

That very same day, Scotland Yard was faced with the fourth mystery death within seven days. A "silent" murder had taken place in a room on the first floor at the back of a house in Regent's Park, within half a mile of the spot where Mabel was found. The latest victim was Edith Humphries. She was discovered clad in her nightdress, shortly after 8.00am, sprawled across a bed in a back room. She had suffered horrendous head wounds. Her dog was found locked in a cupboard. She was rushed to hospital, barely alive, where eminent brain surgeon Dr Guy Rigby Jones decided on an operation with a million-to-one chance of success, in a desperate attempt to save her life. The operation failed. No one had been aware of the attack on the widow until a woman living in a room above came downstairs and saw her lying on the bed.

It was announced by police that they had traced the taxi driver who had taken the man from the house where Theodora Greenhill was strangled, and he was able to give them valuable information. The trunk and items belonging to Mrs Greenhill were found in a suburb in Birmingham. Chief Inspector Salisbury, who had been in the city searching for the suspect, returned to London in the company of Dr Harold Trevor, who was then charged with Theodora's murder. The 61-year-old, described as an architect, was remanded by West London magistrates on 20th October until 4th November. The Chief Inspector alleged that Trevor stated: "After I hit her my mind went completely blank and is still like that now." He added: "It is not murder, Mr Salisbury. There was never any intent of murder."

By 28th October 1941, police were scouring parks and refuse sites in central London for a soldier's battledress which they believed would provide clues in the case of Mabel's murder. It was thought that the battledress – contained in a parcel – had been dumped within the previous fortnight.

At the end of January 1942, murderer Harold Trevor expressed his sympathy for the daughters of his victim at the Old Bailey. "If my life is of any satisfaction to them, then they can take it," he said. He was sentenced to death for the murder of Theodora Jessie Greenhill, but made a long speech before sentence was passed by Mr Justice Asquith. He said: "I am not afraid of anyone, or of what anyone can do. My life up to the age of 62 has been all winter." Trevor was known for "his way with women", and he was described as "suave". He bought a monocle to "add to his charms" and obtained his expensive clothing fraudulently. He had little difficulty in persuading women to fall for him, and bluffed them into believing he was a man of position. They all gave him money. He had 10 aliases, including Sir Francis Ford, Commander Hillier, Captain Gurney and Sir Charles Warren. During his time in prison for fraud in 1925, Trevor had persuaded the Home Secretary – the late Lord Brentford – to visit him. As a result he was released, although he was later sentenced again. It was announced on 31st January that he would appeal against his sentence.

In Mabel's case, the coroner's jury recorded a verdict of murder by person or persons unknown.

# Babes in the Wood
1941

Doreen Hearne (8), described as a pretty child with fair hair and blue eyes, and Kathleen Trendell (6), who lived just a few doors away, disappeared at around 4.30pm in November 1941. They were thought to have accepted the offer of a lift from some soldiers. They were last seen by schoolfriends getting into an army lorry a few hundred yards from their home in Penn, near High Wycombe. It was common for soldiers to drive village children around so no one took much notice, but when the girls didn't arrive home their families began to worry. Mr and Mrs Hearne, together with Mrs Trendell, sat up through the night waiting for news. Mr Trendell was away with the army in India. Scotland Yard was said to be working with Buckinghamshire police to solve the mystery of what happened to the two children. For three nights a "fruitless" search for the girls provided no clues, and fears were expressed for the safety of the girls on 22nd November.

The parents of the children joined the police, Home Guard and wardens in the search of the surrounding countryside. Police believed that the driver of the lorry might have put the children down near their homes, but that they wandered off in the gathering dusk. It was bitterly cold at night and there was concern whether the girls could cope in their clothes, which would hardly keep out the night frost, as well as the fact that they had no food. Police also said that the army driver was probably worried about coming forward, as it was against army rules to carry passengers. An identity parade was held in a Home Counties military camp, so that children from the small hamlet could try to identify the driver. While the missing girls' mothers, frantic with worry, visited friends and relatives to try and trace their movements on the afternoon they disappeared, Doreen's father helped to search the thick woods and lonely lanes in the district. The police couldn't understand why, if the girls had been "taken in" by "kindly folk", they hadn't come forward to say they had found the children.

By 24th November, the search had turned into a "Babes in the Wood" murder hunt. The two girls had been found murdered, covered with leaves, in a wood at Tylers Green, just a few miles from their home. Mrs Trendell was convinced that the killer was one of the soldiers her daughter had taken out tea for when lorries had stopped in Penn. She told the *Mirror*: "The soldiers billeted in this district adored her. She took them out their cups of tea and she knew them all by name. But I believe one of them may be the man who killed Kathleen and Doreen." Widespread inquiries were stepped up at army camps, and drivers' records, journeys and petrol consumption were checked. After the children were driven away in the lorry, nothing more had been seen or heard of them until their bodies were discovered in the wood. Both their throats had been cut and one of them had been stabbed several times. It was also believed that Doreen had been sexually assaulted. The police established that the children were dead before they were flung into the undergrowth. Chief Inspector Hatherill from Scotland Yard and Sir Bernard Spilsbury visited the wood while police searched the area for the murder weapon.

At the end of November 1941, hundreds of weeping children attended the church in Tylers Green to say goodbye at a special memorial service held for the two murdered girls. Police mingled with the crowd, many of whom could not get into the church. Margaret and Ronnie Trendell occupied a front pew alongside Doreen's family. The two children were buried in one grave lined with evergreens and chrysanthemums. No new developments were revealed by police at this time, but on 1st December, Harold Hill (27), a driver in the Royal Artillery, was charged at Chesham with both murders. He had been in the army since just after the outbreak of war. He was interviewed by Chief Inspector Hatherill at his camp and later detained. Meanwhile, the search for the murder weapon continued.

In court, Mr Paling, prosecuting Gunner Hill, said the girls had not been killed where they were found. Sir Bernard said that Doreen had suffered four neck wounds and six stab wounds in the chest; Kathleen had suffered 11 stab wounds in the neck. Hill denied he was out of his camp at the time the girls went missing, but Paling told the court that a partial fingerprint had been retrieved from a gas mask case belonging to one of the children. It was proved to have come from the middle finger of Hill's left hand. "On the radiator of his truck," added Counsel, "Hill had entwined a red poppy. The truck that took away those little girls had such a poppy on its radiator." Major John Carew Jones gave evidence with regard to the identification parades – there were two in total – and in reply to Mr Elborne, defending, agreed that at the first parade, four of five children had failed to identify Hill. The *Mirror* reported on 16th January 1942 that the "babes" murder was not in fact a sex crime. It transpired that neither of the victims had been assaulted, Sir Bernard having revealed his evidence at the hearing in Chesham.

Hill was committed for trial at the Old Bailey, charged with both murders. In March 1942, three women kissed each other outside the Old Bailey. For two days Mrs Hearne and Mrs Trendell had sat on one side of the court, while Hill's mother, Mrs Williams, sat on the other. Between them in the dock sat the accused. He was found guilty of the murder of Doreen. Mrs Williams sat unmoved in court, alone and unsupported, but when the grim verdict was pronounced the two mothers from Penn approached Mrs Williams, and Mrs Trendell said: "I'm so sorry. We have no malice towards you at all. We are mothers ourselves and you have all our sympathy." "It is terrible for you, we know how you must feel," said Mrs Hearne, taking the killer's mother in her arms. Mrs Williams was overwhelmed, and thanked the two ladies. The *Mirror* wrote: "Three women left the court, each with tragedy in her heart. But there was a bond of the deepest sympathy between them."

# Murder in War-Torn Britain

## 1942

Police investigated two murders in early February 1942. The first victim was a woman found strangled in a London air raid shelter. The other woman was found in Victoria Park, Southport, Lancashire, and was identified as Maria Osliff (28), a nurse. A day later, the electric meter man called at a first-floor room in Wardour Street, Soho, London, on 2$^{nd}$ February. There was no answer to his repeated knocking, so he and a woman neighbour pushed the door open. They saw Nita Ward lying across the bed. She was wearing nothing but a short jacket and what seemed to be a red scarf around her neck. But, it wasn't a red scarf. Nita Ward had been brutally murdered, and her throat cut by a tin opener that was found bloodstained in the room with the murder victim. The 32-year-old, whose real name was Mrs Evelyn Oatley, was fascinated by life in the West End of London. On the Monday night before she was found, her radio had been blaring out and disturbing many of her neighbours, who now wondered if it had been put on deliberately to drown the sound of her cries. Divisional Detective Inspector Gray from C Division was put in charge of the case, and immediately ordered his men to begin taking statements from people in Soho clubs.

The police now had three murdered women in two days to investigate. The woman found in the air raid shelter had been identified as Mrs Evelyn Margaret Hamilton (35), a chemist from Hornchurch, Essex, who had recently left her job and her room, telling her landlady that she was moving to Grimsby.

The next victim to be found was Mrs Susan Wilkinson (43), who had her head battered in a lonely lane near her home. Police were alerted by her husband, who became alarmed when she did not return home after a visit to a doctor's house. Another woman had been attacked in the same lane a week before, but she had screamed and her attacker had fled. By 14th February, two more women were dead, found strangled in the West End of London. Mrs Margaret Lawe (45) was found in a flat in Gosfield Street, West London. The week before she had been assaulted by a Canadian soldier, but refused to bring charges. An hour after Margaret's body had been found, Mrs Doris Jouannet (32), wife of a hotel manager, was found at a flat in Sussex Gardens, not far away.

On 17th February a man was charged at Bow Street in London with the murders of Doris, Margaret and Nita. He was named as leading aircraftman in the RAF Gordon Frederick Cummins (28), who was remanded. However, a fresh jury had to be called in April 1942 when a document was handed to the jury by mistake; it was thought that it could prejudice the case. Cummins was dubbed by the press as the "most notorious killer since Jack the Ripper", and a newspaper headline on 29th April read: "Ripper Gets Sentence of Death". He was sentenced to death at the gallows at the Old Bailey, where the jury heard how, according to Mr Justice Asquith, he had killed Nita Ward in a "sadistic sexual murder of a ghoulish type". Cummins had used a safety razor blade to hack at her throat until she was virtually dead, and while she lay dying, gasping for her last breaths, he used a tin opener to gash and mutilate her.

The murders by Cummins had given Scotland Yard its

biggest murder hunt in more than 50 years. Women decoys were employed to trap the ripper killer, but on 13th February, the murderer had given up his identity when he tried to claim another victim, Greta Heywood, in a Haymarket air raid shelter. As the woman screamed, he left behind his gas mask, with his name and service number. Mrs Heywood ran to a police station and the respirator was soon found. That wasn't all he left behind. Cummins' fingerprints were found on a mirror in Nita Ward's room, as well as the tin opener. Newspapers dubbed Cummins a "modern" ripper. He was executed at Wandsworth Prison in London on 25th June 1942.

# The Murder of Caroline Ellen Trayler

## 1943

Caroline Trayler (18), a Folkestone usherette, was found dead in an empty bomb-damaged shop four days after she was reported missing in June 1943. She had been strangled, established the post-mortem examination. That was about the only thing that police had to go on, the *Mirror* was told by Superintendent F.H. Smeed from Kent CID. He confirmed that a speedy solution to the murder was unlikely. The body had been found by a constable detailed to search unoccupied premises following the report that a girl was missing after leaving the Central Cinema where she worked. When the officer went to a door at the rear of a shop in Foord Road, he was only able to push it open a few inches because of its disuse, but he forced his way in and then came to another door leading to the shop and living premises. This door wasn't locked, and on opening it he noticed a woman's blue suede shoe and a brown handbag. A few feet down the passage he saw a body, lying face down with the head resting on the left arm. There was no sign of a struggle or "interference", and it was believed that Caroline had entered the building voluntarily with someone she knew. At the time the murder was committed, the girl's father Frederick Stapleton was on fire watch in a building less than 100 yards from the scene of the crime. Piecing together Caroline's movements, the police ascertained that after leaving the cinema she had visited a local pub, where she was seen talking to a soldier. At the inquest that opened on 18th June, Mr Stapleton identified the dead girl as his daughter. The inquest was then adjourned until 30th June.

Police questioned a number of soldiers for clues about why the crime had been committed and who could be responsible. Smeed and other officers followed a line of inquiry outside Folkestone, and the *Mirror* learned that valuable information had been given in the previous 24 hours concerning the murdered woman's movements in the four days between when she disappeared and when her body was found. Detective Inspector Pierce arrived in Manchester on 22nd June, following information that 24-year-old

Gunner Dennis Edmund Leckey of the Royal Artillery would be able to help with the inquiry. Soon after he reached the city, he received word that Leckey had been staying with a friend in Stoke-on-Trent. The inspector headed for the town immediately. Leckey, who was married, also had relatives in Ashton-under-Lyne, Lancashire, and the police took statements from all of them in an attempt to throw light on his movements. Leckey, it was reported, had been absent from his unit.

Leckey was charged with Caroline's murder on 30th June 1943. He was detained in the West End of London by officers of the US military police and taken to Folkestone, where he appeared before magistrates. He was remanded until 22nd July. Smeed told reporters that he proposed calling evidence of charging Leckey, and then asked for a remand of three weeks to enable the necessary evidence to be submitted to the Director of Prosecutions. After some hesitation, it was alleged that Leckey said: "Well, I have nothing to say until I've seen someone – a solicitor." He was granted legal aid by the magistrate. Stray hairs and particles of dust found on Caroline's body were said to be identical to samples taken from Leckey, it was disclosed in July 1943. He was committed for trial at the Old Bailey.

Dr Keith Simpson, a pathologist, said that on the girl's body he had found six dark hairs entirely different from her hair, which was red. There was a fresh tear in the left first fingernail and underneath it was a wool fibre. This was microscopically identical in colour, size and general character with fibre from a khaki shirt that was said to belong to Leckey. Mr E.G. Robey, prosecuting, said the scientific evidence would show that dark hairs found on the girl's body were identical with Leckey's hairs. In addition, one of Caroline's hairs was found on the accused's trousers. The victim and the accused had also been seen together in the pub the night she died. It was suggested by the prosecution that Leckey had tried to hide his identity. Four soldiers' pay books were found in his possession, and his picture was found in one of them, which belonged to his roommate. Gunner Fred Latham said that Leckey slept in the bed next to him in camp. He told his roommate that he had read about the murder in Folkestone, but Bombardier Kenneth Knight said that he was in the pub with the accused when Caroline came in. He left Leckey with Caroline and didn't see the accused again until the following day. Leckey told him he had kissed the girl but that she had a date to keep, and he had left her shortly after.

At the Old Bailey in September 1943, Leckey told the court: "I love my wife – I love her very much." Answering a question from John Flowers, KC, he said that his reason for going home on "French leave" the weekend after the murder was to tell his wife that he had been unfaithful. He confirmed that he had had a conversation with Caroline in the pub before they left together, but that the first he knew about the murder was when he and four other soldiers were told about it by a barmaid. This was when he decided to confess to his wife. However, later, when he travelled to Stoke, he met Winifred Woolley, and they went to Birmingham where they slept together before moving on to London. He was found guilty by the Old Bailey jury and sentenced to death, but instructed his legal counsel to lodge an appeal against the conviction.

Leckey walked out of the Law Courts a free man on 1st November 1943. He had appealed on five points against the directions by Mr Justice Singleton to the jury. Four of his five points were dismissed by three Appeal Court judges, but on the fifth point they found in his favour. He was taken into custody again to await a military escort from a London barracks, but he was allowed a short meeting with his brother, Military Police Corporal Kenneth Leckey, before being taken to the barracks to face a charge of being an absentee from the army. "He was too overcome to speak to me," Kenneth told the *Mirror*. "He just looked at me smiling and gripped my hand, but he said nothing." In the Appeal Court, Mr J.D. Casswell, KC, for Leckey, pointed out that the judge in his summing up commented on the fact that when cautioned by the police Leckey did not deny the charge, but said he would take advice. What the judge had implied to the jury was that by not denying his innocence, Leckey was as good as admitting his guilt. The Appeal judges felt that the Old Bailey judge's comments on Leckey's silence amounted to a misdirection.

# Arthur Heys
## 1944

Leading Aircraftman Arthur Heys (37) was remanded at Beccles, Suffolk, on 6th December 1944 charged with the murder of Winifred Mary Evans (27), a WAAF from Acton Lane in Harlesden, northwest London. The young woman was found strangled at an RAF camp. Heys, who was married with three children, was reported as living at Harold Street, Colne, Lancashire. On 10th January 1945, the Beccles court was told that "tremendous violence" caused the death of Winifred. Heys' wife sat at the back of the crowded courtroom, and heard how Winifred was found in a ditch in Ellough with her clothes disarranged and torn, bearing signs of the "most brutal handling". Death was caused by suffocation. Found around the young woman's neck was a black tie in a sailor's knot. The case against Heys, who was stationed at the same RAF camp as the dead woman, was that he had been along the road between the WAAF site and the lane where the body was found at the same time as Winifred. It was alleged that coloured brick fragments on his shoes were similar to those found on Miss Evans' shoes. Experts were expected to say that two human bloodstains on his tunic looked as if they came from the victim, who had a different blood group from the accused. Five hairs found on his trousers were, as far as the experts could tell, identical with those from the victim, the court was told.

On 23rd January, the *Mirror* reported that an anonymous letter, written in block capitals, which purported to say that the wrong man was being accused of the murder, was said to have been sent by the accused. The court at Suffolk Assizes held at Bury St Edmunds heard John Flowers, KC, say that Heys had been taken to Norwich prison and brought before magistrates on 10th January. The day before, the anonymous communication had been sent to the CO at the aerodrome bearing a Norwich postmark. Two of Heys' leave forms were in block capitals, filled in by the accused himself. Expert evidence, said Mr Flowers, would be called to confirm that the capital letters were written by one and the same person. The letter read: "Just listen. Will you give this letter to the solicitors for the airman what is so wrongfully accused of murdering Winnie Evans. I want to state that I am the person responsible for the above mentioned girl's death. I had arranged to meet her. I must have been mad and I don't know what happened … I shall be going overseas shortly. Please convey my humble apologies to the airman concerned."

The hearing was adjourned. But on 25th January 1945, the *Mirror* reported that the letter Heys had faked to save his life was in fact sending the murderer to his death. The letter that he had managed to have smuggled out of prison was an important link in the evidence against him. He was sentenced to death after John Flowers, prosecuting, drew attention to a passage stating that a friend had offered to accompany Miss Evans because an airman who was drunk and had lost his way was ahead, – following a dance at the RAF base. "Nobody in the world could have put this in the letter except this man," said the prosecutor. "There was only one man drunk and lost, and that was the prisoner." Mr Justice Macnaghten described it as "a murder more savage and horrible than any in my experience of crime".

Arthur Heys appealed against his sentence to death, and this was heard at the High Court towards the end of February. It was dismissed. Heys was executed in Norwich jail on 13th March 1945.

# WAAF Found Murdered
## 1944

Stripped naked except for her stockings and pink-tinted corsets, an attractive 21-year-old WAAF was found murdered on 14th February 1944 on an allotment in Eltham, southeast London. The young woman was later identified as LACW Iris Deeley. She was found lying face down with her left cheek half-buried in the loose earth. She had been strangled. Bruises and marks were clearly visible on her neck where the assailant had gripped her throat with bare hands. Near her body was a paperback book which the girl had been carrying, and a few yards further on were her service cap and gloves. Her clothing, some of it torn and ripped, was piled clumsily on her body. She had apparently been dragged about 40 yards across the rough surface of the allotment before being violated by her murderer.

It was just after 8.30am when Arthur Belcher, a Southern Railway policeman who lived a stone's throw away, found the body. He phoned the police, and within a short time, Superintendent Rawlings, with Divisional Detective Inspector Green and Detective Inspector Leeming from Eltham CID, was on the scene. Dr Milton, the divisional police surgeon, carried out an examination with a colleague at the spot where the dead girl lay, and estimated that she had been dead for at least six hours. The police then followed up the theory that a soldier might be the murderer. A search along the railway embankment running parallel with the allotment revealed a soldier's khaki glove partially hidden in the short grass, which corresponded with another found close to the murdered woman. People living in the row of houses adjoining the allotment said they had heard what sounded like a scream in the middle of the night. Alfred Hayes, a council employee, told the *Mirror*: "I heard someone shout about two o'clock this morning. It sounded like a shrill cry. It was a woman's voice. I thought no more about it at the time, but now I feel sure it must have been the girl crying out when she was attacked." Plaster casts were taken of footprints that suggested the murderer was wearing heavy boots similar to Army issue. Dr Arthur Davis, a Harley Street pathologist, was set to carry out the post-mortem. It transpired that Iris had been robbed during the attack, and £14 was discovered to be missing from her pockets, together with her cigarette case and Ronson lighter and a book of clothing coupons in the name of her fiancé, Pilot Officer Bill Quill. Iris had only been in Eltham for three weeks – having moved there from South Wales – before she was attacked. Police looked in minute detail at the diary the dead woman had kept, scouring for clues. Quill was away on a training course in the centre of London when he heard about the murder, and was immediately granted 48 hours' compassionate leave. He was then interviewed by police, and was said to be distraught at the loss of his love.

Iris, it transpired, had been known to many as Miriam. An aircraftman in South Wales told the *Mirror* that Miriam was "one of the sweetest and prettiest girls one could wish to meet, and everyone was fond of her". The engagement ring which she had only worn for a week was the only article of value left on her body. Meanwhile, police began a tour of jewellers and pawnbrokers trying to trace her cigarette case, which bore the initials DD. The inquest, opened at Lewisham, was adjourned.

Witnesses reported seeing Iris with a soldier who was wearing a large number of medal ribbons on his tunic. Gunner Ernest James Harman Kemp (21) was arrested on 22nd February when PC Charles Memory noticed that the soldier was wearing medal ribbons for campaigns that took place before Kemp had even been born. It was soon established that Kemp was currently AWOL after absconding from his military escort on 8th February, while under arrest.

On 23rd February, Gunner Kemp was charged with Iris' murder. He was remanded until 13th March after replying: "None at all, sir," when a magistrate asked him if he had any questions. His only known relatives, an uncle and aunt, knew nothing of his arrest until a neighbour knocked on their door to tell them after reading the evening newspaper. Statements Kemp made with regard to Iris' death were read in court in Greenwich in mid-March. He pleaded not guilty and reserved his defence. Mr E. Clayton, prosecuting, said that Iris, who had been on weekend leave, caught a train to Lewisham and was walking to Kidbrooke where she was stationed. On the way she got into conversation with Kemp. He said in a statement that he had put his hand on the woman and she had knocked it away. He could see she was frightened, so he put his hand over her mouth and pulled her to the ground. She tried to struggle, and Kemp described how he twisted her scarf round her neck and pulled it too tight. She "went out and I felt her heart and found she was gone", he said. "I got the wind up and dragged her into the cabbages and left her. I took all her clothes off but did not interfere with her."

Kemp was found guilty of the murder on 18th April at the Old Bailey and sentenced to death. Mr Justice Cassels said the strong recommendation to mercy by the jury would be forwarded to the proper quarter. Summing up, the judge said the jury might think the girl died probably in defence of her honour. Referring to a suggestion of manslaughter, the judge recalled that Kemp had said that he twisted the scarf around her neck and pulled. He asked the jury if they could believe that there was no intention to kill or to seriously injure the victim. An appeal was lodged later in April, but the Court of Criminal Appeal dismissed it.

# The Cleft Chin Murder

1944

A man, robbed of almost every clue to his identity, was found shot dead, with a bullet in his back, in a ditch at Knoll Green, Staines, Middlesex, in October 1944. Scotland Yard combed laundries in order to trace a laundry mark – 202 or 302 – found on his handkerchief, and black ink marks, E 83 (81) and IM 202/468, which were found on his underwear. Tyremarks from a car were found near the ditch. The dead man was described as between 40 and 45 with a cleft chin and dark brown hair, which was curly and well greased. A patch of skin disease was in the process of healing behind the victim's right ear and he had ink stains on the fingers of his right hand. The man was well dressed in utility clothing, including a navy blue overcoat, grey chalk-striped suit, with a blue shirt, tie and socks.

The man was identified on 9th October as George Heath (35) of Kennington Park Road, southeast London, whom it was believed might have upset an inkwell as he fell from his desk. The theory of a fall was supported by evidence that appeared to indicate that the man was murdered in a different location to the one in which he was found. Police believed that he had been taken to Staines by car. At that point, no one had come forward, despite an appeal for anyone who had heard shooting in the early hours on the day of the murder.

An American soldier was the first to be interviewed over the case of the man with the cleft chin. Heath's car – a Ford V8 – was found in the Fulham area following the murder, while an assault summons, Gill versus Heath, was found to involve the dead man and the landlord of a public house, William Gill. The incident had taken place when a barmaid working for Gill had asked the landlord to accompany her to her lodgings, as she wanted to avoid George Heath. Heath's defence was that Gill had struck him first, knocking him down some basement steps before the landlord's dog was let loose on him.

The police retrieved the revolver that had been used to shoot Heath on 13th October 1944 and an arrest appeared imminent. The victim's death was the 16th murder since 1st September, and nightclubs in London's Piccadilly square mile vowed not to use freelance drivers to pick up their patrons in the early hours of the morning. One nightclub owner told the newspapers that: "After this case, we are having regular firms only here as a safeguard."

The American soldier, Private Karl G. Hulten (22) of Boston, Massachusetts, appeared before magistrates at Feltham, Middlesex, on 15th November 1944 charged with the murder of George Heath. In addition, Elizabeth Marina Jones, an 18-year-old blonde dancer, appeared on remand the following day charged with being concerned with him in the murder of the victim. The US Army authorities announced that Hulten had been charged with the murder, but that he would not be tried by court martial until the case against Jones had been concluded.

It was the first time that a British civilian and an American serviceman had been concerned in a capital charge, and British civil and American military authorities worked together to solve the issues raised by the unusual situation. Then, on 16th November 1944, the case made legal history when the American serviceman and the British civilian were brought together in a British court, charged jointly with murder. At Feltham Magistrates Court, Hulten and Jones, from Hammersmith, were charged with being concerned together in the murder of George Heath, taxi driver, known as the man with the cleft chin. Without any evidence being given, both were remanded.

On 27th November, Morgan demonstrated for the prosecution how Heath had been killed by a passenger sitting behind him in his taxi. He stated that the killing was: "a deliberate, cold-blooded act". Jones was described in court as a striptease artist at a nightclub who was married, although her husband was serving abroad. She met Hulten in Hammersmith, where the paratrooper had been frequenting nightclubs, cafés and bars, and the two soon hooked up and became lovers. According to a statement by Jones, she and Hulten – who claimed to be both an officer and a Chicago gangster – left her room on 6th October with the avowed intention of stopping a taxi and robbing the driver.

In Kensington, opposite Cadby Hall, Jones stopped the taxi driven by Heath, who agreed to drive the couple to the end of King's Road, Hammersmith, for 10s. At the end of Chiswick

Road, Hulten told him to stop, and Heath leant over from his seat to open the rear door for Jones. While he was doing so, he was shot in the back, said the prosecution. The bullet then struck the door and ricocheted on to the dashboard. Dr Teare, the prosecution expert, surmised that the victim was shot by someone sitting behind him, and that he would have died within a quarter of an hour of being shot. The victim was then pushed into the passenger seat, and Hulten took his place at the wheel.

While Heath was dying, Jones rifled through the victim's pockets and robbed him of everything he had of value which amounted to £4 in notes in his wallet, about £1 in change from his pockets, a watch and a pen. Once the man was dead, the couple dumped him in a quiet spot before driving back to London in the victim's car. They threw the bullet from the car on the way back to the city and abandoned the car in Fulham, after carefully wiping their prints from the vehicle. That night, the couple stayed together at the girl's room.

When the case came to trial at the Old Bailey, there was a rush for tickets in the cleft chin murder – but the gallery of the court was closed to the public and there were only 40 seats available, which were given on a first come, first served basis. A spokesman for the Old Bailey confirmed that the court never reserved seats for cases and certainly never sold tickets for entry.

On 17th January 1945, a deathly pale girl sat drooping and motionless in a brightly lit court at the Old Bailey while Counsel read a statement that she was alleged to have made to the

American paratrooper. It read: "I would like to do something exciting – like becoming a gun moll, like they do in the States." While there was a rustle in the courtroom to hear the statement, said to have been made by Hulten about small-town Welsh girl Jones, the accused, who was once described as "a lovely blonde" but now "worn out, sick and broken", seemingly showed no interest in her fate. All through that day, she sat motionless.

Lenny Bexley, a diminutive man who had gone to the dogs with Hulten and Jones on the day following the shooting, went into the box to describe the progress of the couple's friendship. When the revolver used in the shooting was brought up in court, Bexley confirmed that Hulten had been immensely proud of the gun and had showed it to him three times. The accused had even laid it on the table in a Hammersmith café when he sold Bexley the pen that had been taken from the victim. The next witness was Edith Evans from King Street, Hammersmith, who was Jones' landlady. She gave evidence about the comings and goings at her home in the fateful week that Heath was shot, before Maurice Levine, a Hammersmith barber, took the stand to describe how he had come to buy the victim's watch from Hulten on the morning following Heath's death. The next witness was Detective Inspector Percy Reed, who had a fierce technical discussion with Counsel about the revolver.

Lieutenant de Mott, an American Army CID agent, was, for two days in succession, put under a close cross-examination by Hulten's counsel, John Maude. With the judge intervening frequently and Maude repeatedly complaining that he could not hear the witness, de Mott clung rigidly to his testimony. Statements alleged to have been made by Hulten were read, in which the accused said that he had held the gun to his chest when Heath stopped the car, and had intended to shoot straight through the car, when suddenly – just as he pulled the trigger – Heath heaved upwards and sideways in the driving seat in an attempt to open the rear door on the opposite side. The fact that this statement indicated the possibility of an accidental shooting was stressed at great length by the defence. Parts of Hulten's statements were suppressed by general consent, but Maude later recalled de Mott to talk about the one sentence not previously mentioned: that during a conversation between Hulten and Jones, the girl had expressed her wish to do "something exciting" and that she wanted to be a gun moll. The self-proclaimed gangster had obviously been happy to oblige.

Jones' mother, Nellie Baker, was in court one to see her daughter stand trial accused of murder. Dressed in black, Baker sat with her husband in the public seats at the right of the dock and gazed pitifully at her daughter. She told reporters outside the court: "It is so long since I saw her. I did so much want just one little word," which the judge had refused earlier that day in court. In the dock, separated by a policewoman from the frail, grey-coated girl, stood Hulten, short, thick-set, shock-haired, a faint smile half-raising his heavy features. Hulten had been seen to be doodling in court, and it was soon apparent that this was an important point in the case.

Maude fought for two and a half hours to prove that two incriminating statements made by Hulten were inadmissible in an English court. He tried to show that they had been obtained under pressure over an unduly long period, but the prosecution claimed that the accused's doodling between questions and answers were what prolonged the interview conducted by de Mott in the presence of two British detectives. Maude then recalled de Mott yet again to question him about the methods he had used in the interview. But the American Army CID agent quietly refuted any charges of irregularity.

It was 18th January 1945 when Jones hesitantly entered the witness box to tell her side of the story. A hush fell on the courtroom at 2.16pm as she quietly told the events of her 18 years, while accused of murdering Heath jointly with Hulten. With one hand in the pocket of the shabby grey coat that was buttoned high to her neck, Jones stood swaying slightly in the dock. Haltingly, and in a scarcely audible undertone – but with a marked American accent – she began to give the jury an insight into her unhappy life, laid bare by a lack of make-up and peroxide.

She told how she had been born in Wales, but had moved with her family to Canada at the age of three to five years. When Jones was aged 13, the father that she loved deeply was called up, and she told how she had never been happy again. The family had returned to Wales by this time, and on three occasions she had tried to leave home in order to return to her father. She told how, at the age of 16, she married Lance-Bombardier Stanley Jones, who was a paratrooper, that he had struck her on the first night of their marriage and how she had never lived with him. (He was reported missing, believed killed in Arnhem on the day that the accused was charged.) With continued requests from the judge and jury to speak louder, the girl in the dock who had tearfully described herself to policemen as "a bad girl" because she drank so much for her age, told how she had come to London in January 1943, just two months after her marriage. She had worked as a barmaid, an usherette and a café waitress, but in April that year she realized her ambition and found a job as a dancer – a striptease artist in a West End nightclub. Late in 1943, her job as a dancer was over, and she lived on the small army allowance that she received from her husband, from whom she had never formally separated. She was asked by her defence counsel, J. D. Casswell, if she had ever been a prostitute. She breathed sharply and brushed her eyes with the back of her hand before answering loudly: "No, sir."

Questions then turned to the night that George Heath was murdered and the story of the man whom she knew as "Ricky", who sat in the dock starring hard at her. "I thought he was a gentleman," she said bitterly of Karl Hulten. She had allegedly told him that she wanted to do something dangerous, such as flying over Germany, and it was at this point that "Ricky" told her he was a gunman. She told the court that when they got into Heath's car she thought they were going home, but she was too afraid of the American to question him. After Hulten had asked the driver to slow down she saw the gun in his hand, and when the car stopped she heard a shot. She said that she had been ordered to go through the dying man's pockets and that she refused, but Hulten had indicated with the revolver that she should do what he said. He allegedly told Jones: "I will do the same to you if you don't go through his pockets." Jones said that while she was looking through the victim's pockets, he was breathing heavily. She did not help Hulten drag Heath into the ditch. Back in Jones' room she told Hulten that he had committed cold-blooded murder. Asked why, the American had said: "People in my profession are used to things like that. I always get people who inform against me first." Jones declared that when she went on the car journey, she did not know that Hulten intended to rob the driver. However, when Hulten went into the witness box, it was a very different story.

The American paratrooper denied that he had ever been a Chicago gunman; he said he had never even been to the city. The accused also denied that he had ever told Jones that he was a gangster in America and had been running a similar racket in the UK. Asked to explain the events leading up to Heath's death, Hulten said: "We had decided to stop a cab. When I met Miss Jones, I went to her room. She made some remarks about going out that night and robbing a cab. I argued against this and she asked for my gun and said she would go out herself."

Earlier in court under cross-examination, Jones had said:

"He told me that he was a gunman back in Chicago and was operating a gang in London." Jones had also told the court that she was afraid of Hulten, who reminded her several times that he had a loaded gun. She said he had even struck her once when she forgot to ask his permission to go downstairs to have a wash. Jones also declared that Hulten had kept all the money taken from Heath.

While on trial, and held in Holloway prison, North London, Jones had written a dramatic letter to her co-accused saying: "If I get sent to prison it will kill my mother. So you see, Ricky, why you must tell the truth. Don't you think I've suffered enough?" Passages from the letter were read out in court, where both pleaded not guilty of murder. The letter also said: "You promised me in court you would tell the whole truth. Do not go back on your word Ricky." It continued: "What the police have against me is going through the man's pockets. Had you not ordered me to do so I would never have done it. But as my own life was in danger I did so. I could not believe you had done it, Ricky. I did not help you to carry him to the ditch. You know that. Ricky, for God's sake tell the truth. You and God are the only two who know of my innocence. Half of this case is fresh to me. The gun for instance – I did not know it was stolen. I did not know your real name, your age, your right rank. You were posing as an officer. I did not know you were married and had a child. I did not know you had deserted the Army. Why did you do it, Ricky, and why have you got me into this?"

Mr Byrne, counsel for the Crown, was relentless in his cross-examination of Hulten. But when the trial entered its last stage on 23rd January 1945, Maude made a dramatic appeal to the jury of nine men and three women on behalf of the American. He repeated several times: "Charity never faileth." He continued: "I beseech you, see that that little candle does not flicker out." He described Jones as being able to lie just as much as Hulten, and he did not ask the jury to set his client free as he feared that the serviceman was responsible for manslaughter.

In his summing up, Mr Justice Charles reiterated that Hulten had said he did not know that the trigger of the gun was back and the cartridge was in the breech. But he asked the jury if they could believe a word of the story told by Hulten. Shaking his head, the judge said: "The cartridge could not get into the breech by accident. That needs a click." The judge went on to speak of the incredible cold-blooded brutality which followed the shooting, and that Hulten neither knew nor cared whether the victim was alive or dead. The judge described how the victim had had his personal belongings removed from him while he lay dying on the passenger seat of his own car. "Accident? Was that an accident," asked the judge, "or was it murder?" Mr Justice Charles said that the jury were entitled to acquit the woman if they believed that she had been forced into the matter against her will. Referring to the statement that Jones had wanted to be thrilled, the judge said she had found someone to give her a greater thrill than she had ever expected. He also spoke of the letter read to the court, and surmised that Hulten had been intent on drawing the girl into "the net". Towards the close of his summing up, the judge said: "Mr Maude has invited a verdict of manslaughter. I cannot exclude that from your consideration, but I am bound to tell you that the set of circumstances which Mr Maude puts forward as justifying a verdict of manslaughter do not concur with Hulten's description of what happened."

Hulten was convicted of the murder of George Heath and sentenced to death. At the end of January 1945, his family was thinking of appealing against the sentence to President Roosevelt or General Eisenhower. Elizabeth "Betty" Jones was also convicted of murder and sentenced to die. She was held in a heavily barred room at Holloway prison because there was no condemned cell. An appeal for both parties was held on 19th February 1945, where lawyers battled it out to save the convicted couple's lives. Both lost their appeals, and the sentence of death was to stand. Hulten left the courtroom smiling slightly and joking with his guards as his fate was sealed. Jones was led away by two prison guards with no fuss.

The car in which Heath was killed was sold to car dealer George Page in Chippenham, who planned to auction it. He had already had two bids for four-figure sums for the grey coupé, which remained in the hands of Scotland Yard. Both Hulten (held at Pentonville) and Jones (still in Holloway) were sentenced to die on 8th March 1945, but at the end of February, 33,000 people were due to decide if they wished to save the young girl's life.

The people of Neath, Glamorgan – Jones' hometown – received petition forms for her reprieve. Despite the fact that the residents of Neath strongly disapproved of the teenager's way of life, those backing the campaign were not convinced that she should die. It was reported in the press that even the mayor, Thomas Hughes, was considering a formal civic appeal to the Home Secretary. However, messages scrawled on walls in the town declared that Jones should hang. Many of the town's residents declared that either both Hulten and Jones should hang or that both should be reprieved. Arthur Baker (45), Jones' father, had tried in vain to encourage people to sign the petition to save his daughter, but only 200 put pen to paper – mostly married women with daughters of their own; but many also declared that Hulten should be saved as well. In Glasgow, five young women working in a factory walked into the Sheriff's Court on 7th March, protesting against a recommendation by the Home Secretary that Jones should be reprieved.

Hulten spent his last few hours quietly after attending Mass at Wormwood Scrubs. He played chess with his guards before a van drew into the prison yard to take him to Pentonville. He exercised in the afternoon and wrote a farewell letter to his wife. He was not informed that Jones had, in fact, been given a reprieve. As he faced the scaffold on the morning of 8th March, there were scuffles outside Pentonville as a white lorry came hurtling towards the prison gates. A quick-thinking police inspector signalled to a lorry coming up the road to bar the entrance to the prison, and

Home Front Killers

a collision was avoided when the offending lorry swerved. It had been a small protest against capital punishment by Mrs Van der Elst, and she was later charged at Clerkenwell police court of causing grievous bodily harm to Police Sergeant Horace Jarvis.

While Hulten hanged for his part in the murder, Jones was given a life sentence, and her property was placed by magistrates in Neath in the care of her mother. A solicitor confirmed that eventually Jones would be released back into society, whereupon she would inherit the estate of Stanley Jones, her husband, who had been confirmed dead at Arnhem without having made a will. Hulten's and Jones' friendship had only lasted six days after they met on 3rd October 1944. During this time they had knocked over and killed a nurse cycling along a country lane and had also robbed a hitchhiker, whom they knocked unconscious and threw into a river to drown. George Heath had been their final victim in just a few short days of "excitement" for Jones and death and destruction for Hulten. Jones was released from prison in May 1954, but her movements and whereabouts after she regained her freedom are still unknown.

Home Front Killers